Major Railways 主要鉄道

J.R.(Shinkansen) JR新幹線
J.R.(Express) JR特急運行線
J.R.(Local) JR地方線
Other Railways その他の鉄道

D0191376

1 : 4,060,000

0   100   200km

140°

35°

Distributed in the United States by Kodansha America, Inc.,
114 Fifth Avenue, New York, N.Y. 10011.
and in the United Kingdom and continental Europe
by Kodansha Europe Ltd.,
Gillingham House, 38-44 Gillingham Street, London SW1V 1HU.
Published by Kodansha International Ltd., 17-14, Otowa 1-chome,
Bunkyo-ku, Tokyo 112, and Kodansha America, Inc.
Produced by Iris Co.,Ltd., 39-30, Fujimi-cho 1-chome,
Chofu City, Tokyo 182, Japan.

93 94 95 96 97 10 9 8 7 6 5 4 3 2 1

ISBN 4-7700-1781-2

TOKYO METROPOLITAN AREA

RAIL & ROAD

ATLAS

首都圏二ヵ国語交通アトラス

目 次 ──────────────── CONTENTS

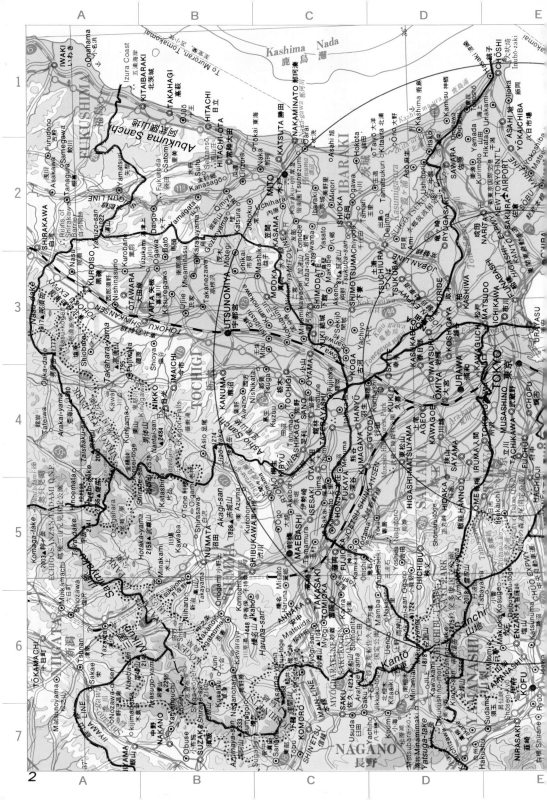

Tokyo Metropolitan Area
首都圏

PACIFIC OCEAN
太 平 洋

TOKYO 東京

Izu - Shotō 伊豆諸島

Sagami Nada 相模灘

Sagami-Wan 相模湾

Suruga Wan 駿河湾

1:1,260,000

0   50km

3

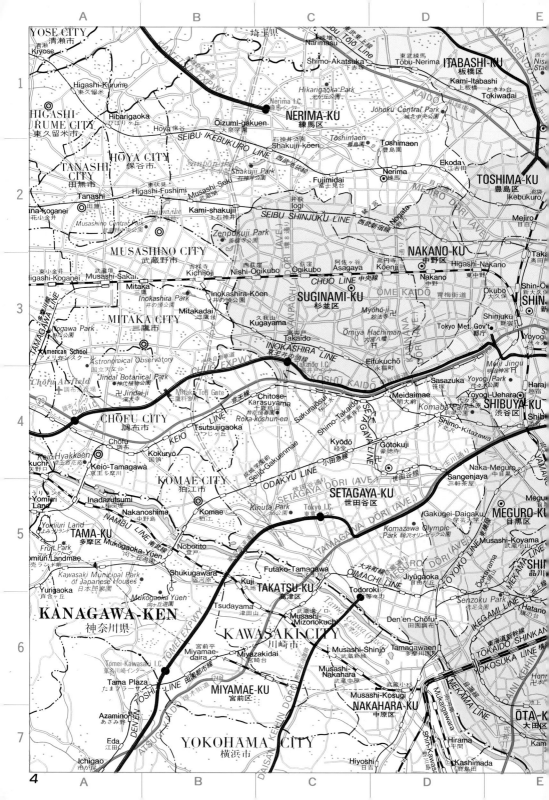

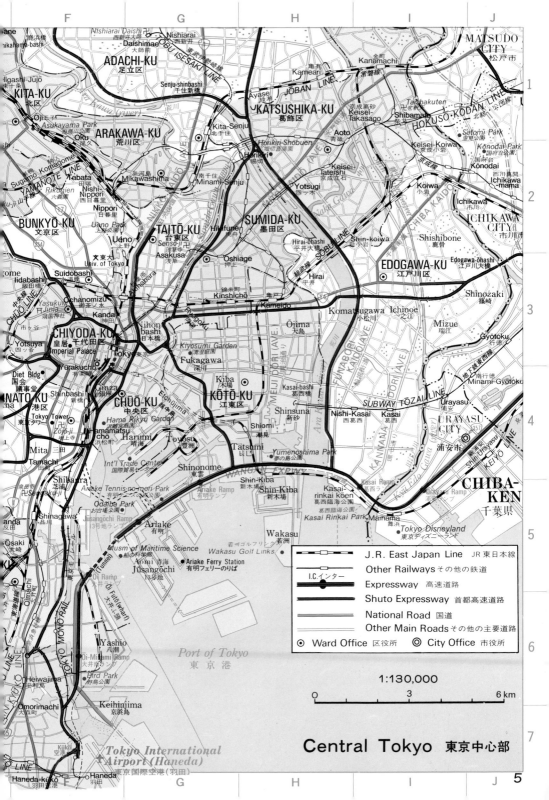

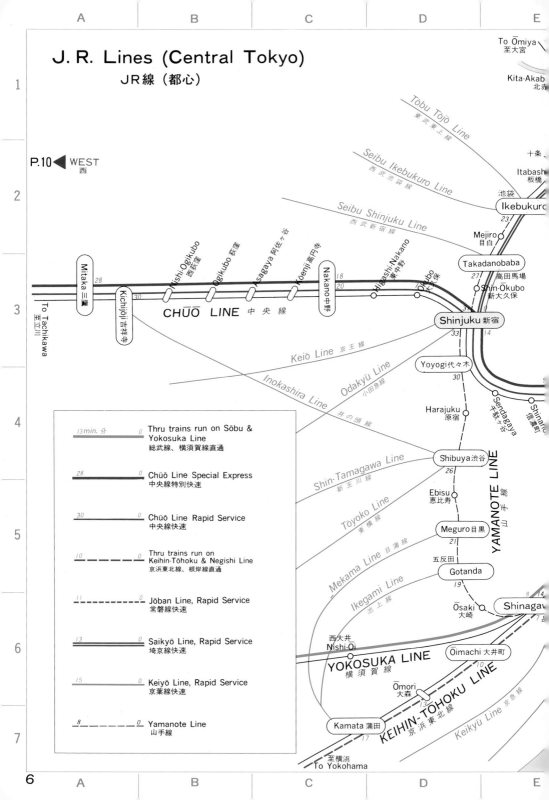

J. R. Lines (Central Tokyo)
JR線（都心）

P.10 ◀ WEST 西

To Ōmiya 至大宮

Kita-Akab 北赤

十条

Itabash 板橋

池袋
Ikebukuro

Tōbu Tōjō Line 東武東上線

Seibu Ikebukuro Line 西武池袋線

Seibu Shinjuku Line 西武新宿線

Mejiro 目白

Takadanobaba 高田馬場

Shin-Ōkubo 新大久保

Mitaka 三鷹

To Tachikawa 至立川

Kichijōji 吉祥寺

Nishi-Ogikubo 西荻窪

Ogikubo 荻窪

Asagaya 阿佐ヶ谷

Kōenji 高円寺

Nakano 中野

Higashi-Nakano 東中野

Ōkubo 大久保

Shinjuku 新宿

CHŪO LINE 中央線

Keiō Line 京王線

Odakyū Line 小田急線

Inokashira Line 井の頭線

Yoyogi 代々木

Harajuku 原宿

Sendagaya 千駄ヶ谷

Shinan 信濃

Shin-Tamagawa Line 新玉川線

Shibuya 渋谷

Ebisu 恵比寿

Tōyoko Line 東横線

Meguro 目黒

Mekama Line 目蒲線

Ikegami Line 池上線

Gotanda 五反田

Ōsaki 大崎

Shinagaw

YAMANOTE LINE 山手線

Nishi-Ōi 西大井

Ōimachi 大井町

YOKOSUKA LINE 横須賀線

Ōmori 大森

Kamata 蒲田

KEIHIN-TŌHOKU LINE 京浜東北線

Keikyū Line 京急線

To Yokohama 至横浜

13min. 分 — 0	Thru trains run on Sōbu & Yokosuka Line 総武線、横須賀線直通
28 — 0	Chūō Line Special Express 中央線特別快速
30 — 0	Chūō Line Rapid Service 中央線快速
10 --- 0	Thru trains run on Keihin-Tōhoku & Negishi Line 京浜東北線、根岸線直通
11 --- 0	Jōban Line, Rapid Service 常磐線快速
13 — 0	Saikyō Line, Rapid Service 埼京線快速
15 — 0	Keiyō Line, Rapid Service 京葉線快速
8 --- 0	Yamanote Line 山手線

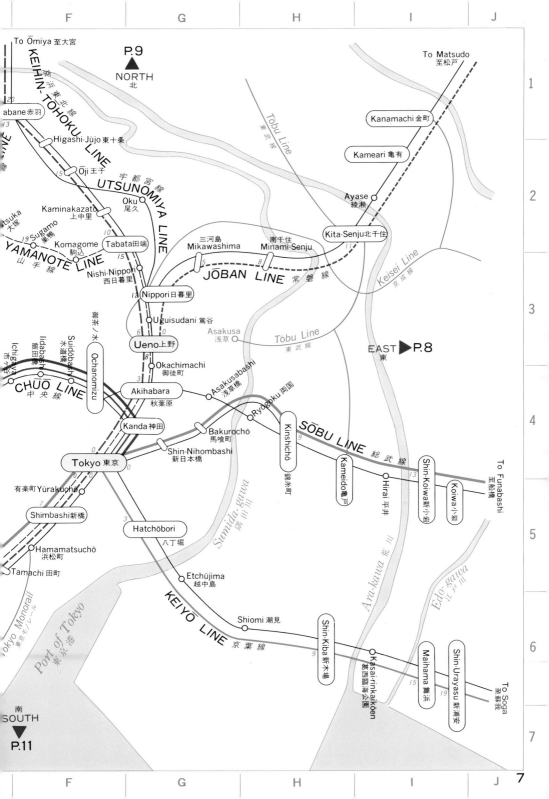

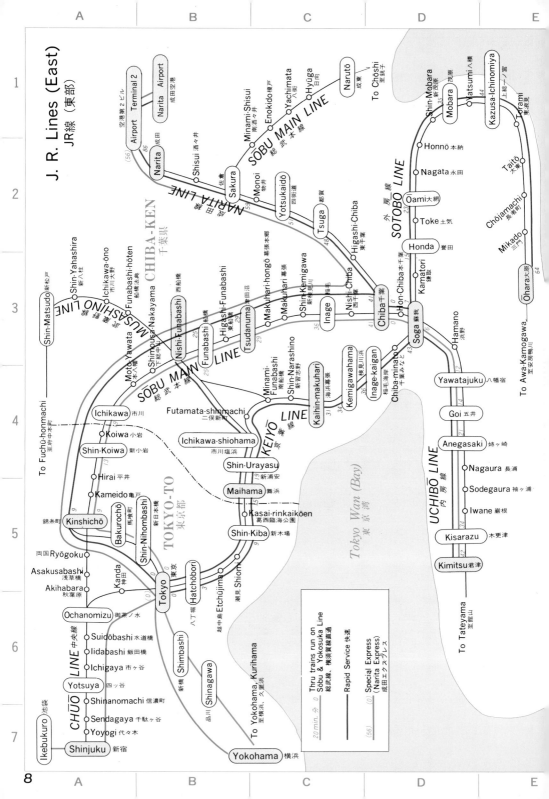

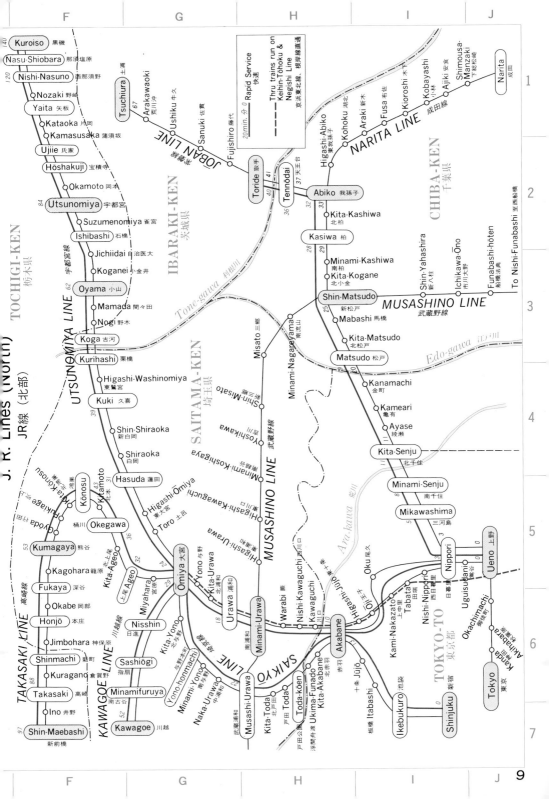

J. R. Lines (North) JR線 (北部)

TOCHIGI-KEN 栃木県

IBARAKI-KEN 茨城県

SAITAMA-KEN 埼玉県

CHIBA-KEN 千葉県

TOKYO-TO 東京都

Kuroiso 黒磯
Nasu-Shiobara 那須塩原
Nishi-Nasuno 西那須野
Nozaki 野崎
Yaita 矢板
Kataoka 片岡
Kamasusaka 蒲須坂
Ujiie 氏家
Hoshakuji 宝積寺
Okamoto 岡本
Utsunomiya 宇都宮
Suzumenomiya 雀宮
Ishibashi 石橋
Jichiidai 自治医大
Koganei 小金井
Oyama 小山
Mamada 間々田
Nogi 野木
Koga 古河
Kurihashi 栗橋
Higashi-Washinomiya 東鷲宮
Kuki 久喜
Shin-Shiraoka 新白岡
Shiraoka 白岡
Hasuda 蓮田

UTSUNOMIYA LINE 宇都宮線

Tsuchiura 土浦
Arakawaoki 荒川沖
Ushiku キ久
Sanuki 佐貫
Fujishiro 藤代
Toride 取手
Tennodai 天王台

JOBAN LINE 常磐線

Higashi-Abiko 東我孫子
Kohoku 湖北
Araki 新木
Fusa 布佐
Kioroshi 木下
Kobayashi 小林
Ajiki 安食
Shimousa-Manzaki 下総松崎
Narita 成田

NARITA LINE 成田線 至西船橋 To Nishi-Funabashi

Abiko 我孫子
Kita-Kashiwa 北柏
Kasiwa 柏
Minami-Kashiwa 南柏
Kita-Kogane 北小金
Shin-Matsudo 新松戸
Mabashi 馬橋
Kita-Matsudo 北松戸
Matsudo 松戸
Kanamachi 金町
Kameari 亀有
Ayase 綾瀬
Kita-Senju 北千住
Minami-Senju 南千住
Mikawashima 三河島

Shin-Yahashira 新八柱
Ichikawa-Ōno 市川大野
Funabashi-hōten 船橋法典

MUSASHINO LINE 武蔵野線

Minami-Nagareyama 南流山
Misato 三郷
Shin-Misato 新三郷
Yoshikawa 吉川
Minami-Koshigaya 南越谷
Higashi-Kawaguchi 東川口
Higashi-Urawa 東浦和

TONE-gawa 利根川
Edo-gawa 江戸川
Ara-kawa 荒川

Oku 尾久
Nippori 日暮里
Ueno 上野
Uguisudani 鶯谷
Nishi-Nippori 西日暮里
Tabata 田端
Kami-Nakazato 上中里
Okachimachi 御徒町
Akihabara 秋葉原
Kanda 神田
Tokyo 東京

TAKASAKI LINE 高崎線

Kuroiso...
Kōnosu 鴻巣
Kitamoto 北本
Okegawa 桶川
Kumagaya 熊谷
Kagohara 籠原
Fukaya 深谷
Okabe 岡部
Honjō 本庄
Jimbohara 神保原
Shinmachi 新町
Kuragano 倉賀野
Takasaki 高崎
Ino 井野
Shin-Maebashi 新前橋

KAWAGOE LINE 川越線

Miyahara 宮原
Nisshin 日進
Sashiōgi 指扇
Minamifuruya 南古谷
Kawagoe 川越

Kita-Ageo 北上尾
Ageo 上尾
Kita-Yono 北与野
Yono 与野
Yono-hommachi 与野本町
Naka-Urawa 中浦和
Minami-Yono 南与野
Musashi-Urawa 武蔵浦和

Omiya 大宮
Kita-Urawa 北浦和
Urawa 浦和
Minami-Urawa 南浦和

SAIKYO LINE 埼京線

Warabi 蕨
Nishi-Kawaguchi 西川口
Kawaguchi 川口
Akabane 赤羽
Higashi-Jūjō 東十条
Ōji 王子
Jūjō 十条
Itabashi 板橋
Shin-Akabane 新赤羽
Kita-Akabane 北赤羽
Ukima-Funado 浮間舟渡
Toda-Kōen 戸田公園
Toda 戸田
Kita-Toda 北戸田

Ikebukuro 池袋
Shinjuku 新宿

Thru trains run on
Keihin-Tohoku &
Negishi Line
京浜東北線、根岸線直通

20 min. 分 → Rapid Service 快速
- - -

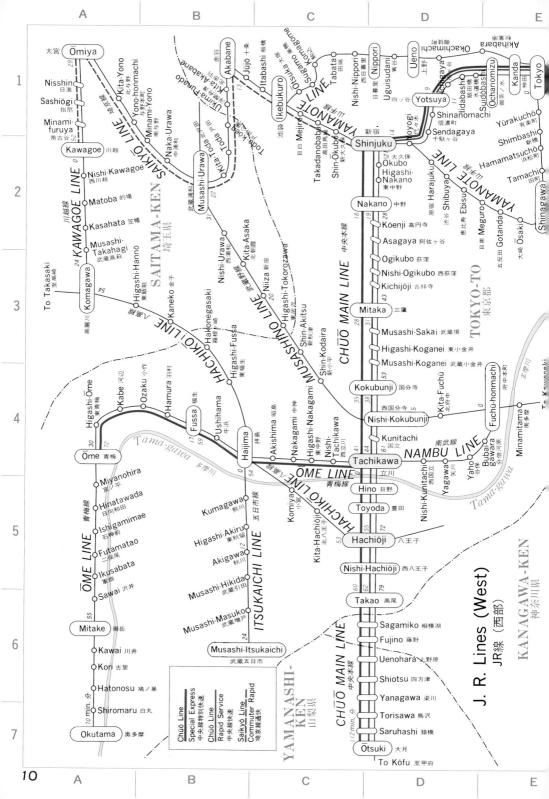

J. R. Lines (West) JR線 (西部)

TOKYO-TO 東京都

SAITAMA-KEN 埼玉県

KANAGAWA-KEN 神奈川県

YAMANASHI-KEN 山梨県

大宮 Ōmiya

Nisshin 日進
Sashiōgi 指扇
Minami-furuya 南古谷
Kawagoe 川越
Nishi-Kawagoe 西川越
Matoba 的場
Kasahata 笠幡
Musashi-Takahagi 武蔵高萩
Komagawa 高麗川

Kita-Yono 北与野
Yono-honmachi 与野本町
Minami-Yono 南与野
Naka-Urawa 中浦和
Musashi-Urawa 武蔵浦和
Nishi-Urawa 西浦和
Kita-Asaka 北朝霞
Niiza 新座
Higashi-Tokorozawa 東所沢
Shin-Akitsu 新秋津

SAIKYŌ LINE
KAWAGOE LINE 川越線
HACHIKŌ LINE 八高線
MUSASHINO LINE 武蔵野線

To Takasaki 至高崎

Higashi-Hannō 東飯能
Kaneko 金子
Hakonegasaki 箱根ヶ崎
Higashi-Fussa 東福生
Kabe 河辺
Ozaku 小作
Hamura 羽村
Fussa 福生
Ushihama 牛浜
Haijima 拝島
Akishima 昭島
Nakagami 中神
Higashi-Nakagami 東中神
Nishi-Tachikawa 西立川

Higashi-Ōme 東青梅
Ōme 青梅
Miyanohira 宮ノ平
Hinatawada 日向和田
Ishigamimae 石神前
Futamatao 二俣尾
Ikusabata 軍畑
Sawai 沢井
Mitake 御岳
Kawai 川井
Kori 古里
Hatonosu 鳩ノ巣
Shiromaru 白丸
Okutama 奥多摩

ŌME LINE 青梅線

Kumagawa 熊川
Higashi-Akiru 東秋留
Akigawa 秋川
Musashi-Hikida 武蔵引田
Musashi-Masuko 武蔵増戸
Musashi-Itsukaichi 武蔵五日市

ITSUKAICHI LINE 五日市線

Tama-gawa 多摩川

Akabane 赤羽
Jūjō 十条
Itabashi 板橋
Ōtsuka 大塚
Sugamo 巣鴨
Komagome 駒込
Ukima-Funado 浮間舟渡
Kita-Akabane 北赤羽
Ikebukuro 池袋
Mejiro 目白
Takadanobaba 高田馬場
Shin-Ōkubo 新大久保

Tabata 田端
Nishi-Nippori 西日暮里
Nippori 日暮里
Uguisudani 鶯谷
Ueno 上野
Okachimachi 御徒町
Akihabara 秋葉原
Asakusabashi 浅草橋
Kanda 神田
Ochanomizu 御茶ノ水
Suidōbashi 水道橋
Iidabashi 飯田橋
Ichigaya 市ヶ谷
Yotsuya 四ツ谷
Tokyo 東京

YAMANOTE LINE

Shinjuku 新宿
Ōkubo 大久保
Higashi-Nakano 東中野
Nakano 中野
Kōenji 高円寺
Asagaya 阿佐ヶ谷
Ogikubo 荻窪
Nishi-Ogikubo 西荻窪
Kichijōji 吉祥寺
Mitaka 三鷹
Musashi-Sakai 武蔵境
Higashi-Koganei 東小金井
Musashi-Koganei 武蔵小金井
Kokubunji 国分寺
Nishi-Kokubunji 西国分寺
Kunitachi 国立
Tachikawa 立川
Hino 日野
Toyoda 豊田
Hachiōji 八王子
Nishi-Hachiōji 西八王子
Takao 高尾

Yoyogi 代々木
Sendagaya 千駄ヶ谷
Shinanomachi 信濃町
Harajuku 原宿
Shibuya 渋谷
Ebisu 恵比寿
Meguro 目黒
Gotanda 五反田
Ōsaki 大崎
Shinagawa 品川
Tamachi 田町
Hamamatsuchō 浜松町
Shimbashi 新橋
Yūrakuchō 有楽町

CHŪŌ MAIN LINE 中央本線
NAMBU LINE 南武線

Nishi-Kunitachi 西国立
Yagawa 矢川
Yaho 谷保
Bubai-gawara 分倍河原
Minamitama 南多摩
Fuchū-honmachi 府中本町
Kita-Fuchū 北府中

To Kawasaki 至川崎
Tama-gawa 多摩川

Kita-Hachiōji 北八王子
Komiya 小宮
Kita-Hachiōji 北八王子

HACHIKŌ LINE 八高線

Sagamiko 相模湖
Fujino 藤野
Uenohara 上野原
Shiotsu 四方津
Yanagawa 梁川
Torisawa 鳥沢
Saruhashi 猿橋
Ōtsuki 大月

CHŪŌ MAIN LINE 中央本線

To Kōfu 至甲府

Chūō Line
Special Express 中央線特別快速
Chūō Line
Rapid Service 中央線快速
Saikyō Line
Commuter Rapid 埼京線通勤快速

70 min. 分

112 min. 分

10

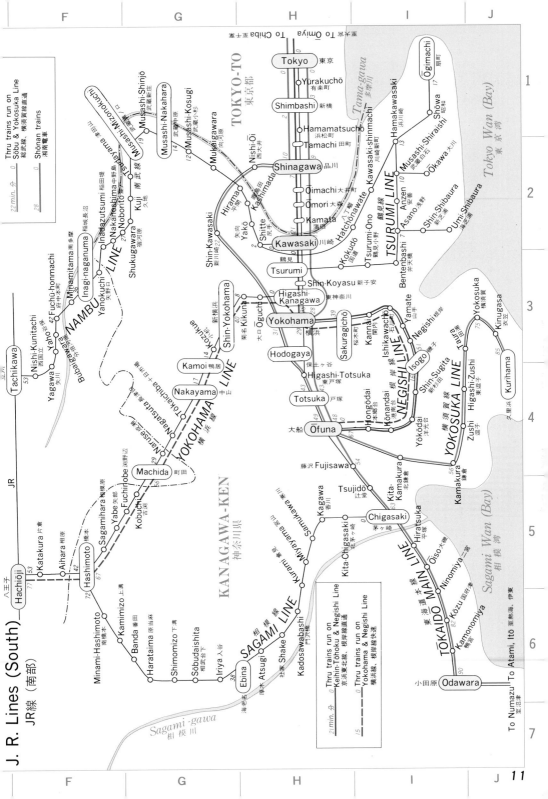

J. R. Lines (South)
JR線 (南部)

Thru trains run on Sōbu & Yokosuka Line 総武線、横須賀線直通

Shonan trains 湘南電車

22 min. 分

28

Thru trains run on Keihin-Tōhoku & Negishi Line 京浜東北線、根岸線直通

Thru trains run on Yokohama & Negishi Line 横浜線、根岸線快速

21 min. 分

15

TOKYO-TO 東京都

KAN AGAWA-KEN 神奈川県

NAMBU LINE

YOKOHAMA LINE

SAGAMI LINE

TSURUMI LINE

NEGISHI LINE

YOKOSUKA LINE

TŌKAIDŌ MAIN LINE

Tama-gawa 多摩川

Sagami-gawa 相模川

Sagami Wan (Bay) 相模湾

Tokyo Wan (Bay) 東京湾

To Fuji Chiba 至木更津 千葉
To Chiba 千葉
To Ōmiya 至大宮 大宮
To Ono 至大野

Tokyo 東京
Yurakuchō 有楽町
Shimbashi 新橋
Hamamatsucho 浜松町
Tamachi 田町
Shinagawa 品川
Ōimachi 大井町
Ōmori 大森
Kamata 蒲田
Kawasaki 川崎
Tsurumi 鶴見
Shin-Koyasu 新子安
Higashi-Kanagawa 東神奈川
Yokohama 横浜
Hodogaya 保土ヶ谷
Higashi-Totsuka 東戸塚
Totsuka 戸塚
Ofuna 大船
Fujisawa 藤沢
Tsujidō 辻堂
Chigasaki 茅ヶ崎
Hiratsuka 平塚
Ōiso 大磯
Ninomiya 二宮
Kōzu 国府津
Kamonomiya 鴨宮
Odawara 小田原

Nishi-Ōi 西大井
Hirama 平間
Kashimada 鹿島田
Mukaigawara 向河原
Shitte 尻手
Yakō 矢向
Shin-Kawasaki 新川崎
Tsurumi-Ono 鶴見小野
Anzen 安善
Asano 浅野
Bentembashi 弁天橋
Hatchōnawate 八丁畷
Kokudō 国道
Umi-Shibaura 海芝浦
Shin-Shibaura 新芝浦
Kawasaki-shinmachi 川崎新町
Musashi-Shiraishi 武蔵白石
Ōkawa 大川
Shōwa 昭和
Hamakawasaki 浜川崎

Ōgimachi 扇町

Musashi-Mizonokuchi 武蔵溝ノ口
Musashi-Shinjō 武蔵新城
Musashi-Nakahara 武蔵中原
Musashi-Kosugi 武蔵小杉
Noborito 登戸
Kuji 久地
Shukugawara 宿河原
Nakanoshima 中野島
Inadazutsumi 稲田堤
Yanokuchi 矢野口
Minamitama 南多摩
Bubaigawara 分倍河原
Yagawa 矢川
Yaho 谷保
Nishi-Kunitachi 西国立
Nishi-Kunitachi
Tachikawa 立川
Katakura 片倉
Aihara 相原
Hashimoto 橋本
Minami-Hashimoto 南橋本
Kamimizo 上溝
Harataima 原当麻
Shimomizo 下溝
Sōbudaishita 相武台下
Iriya 入谷
Ebina 海老名
Atsugi 厚木
Shake 社家
Kadosawabashi 門沢橋
Kita-Chigasaki 北茅ヶ崎
Kagawa 香川
Miyayama 宮山
Samukawa 寒川
Kurami 倉見
Fuchū-honmachi 府中本町

Kikuna 菊名
Kōzukue 小机
Nakayama 中山
Kamoi 鴨居
Machida 町田
Sagamihara 相模原
Yabe 矢部
Fuchinobe 淵野辺
Kobuchi 古淵

Shin-Yokohama 新横浜

Kannai 関内
Sakuragichō 桜木町
Ishikawachō 石川町
Yamate 山手
Negishi 根岸
Isogo 磯子
Shin-Sugita 新杉田
Yōkōdai 洋光台
Konandai 港南台
Hongōdai 本郷台

Yamate 山手
Yokosuka 横須賀
Kinugasa 衣笠
Kurihama 久里浜
Higashi-Zushi 東逗子
Zushi 逗子
Kamakura 鎌倉
Kita-Kamakura 北鎌倉

Fuchū-honmachi 府中本町

To Numazu To Atami, Itō 至沼津 至熱海、伊東

JR

11

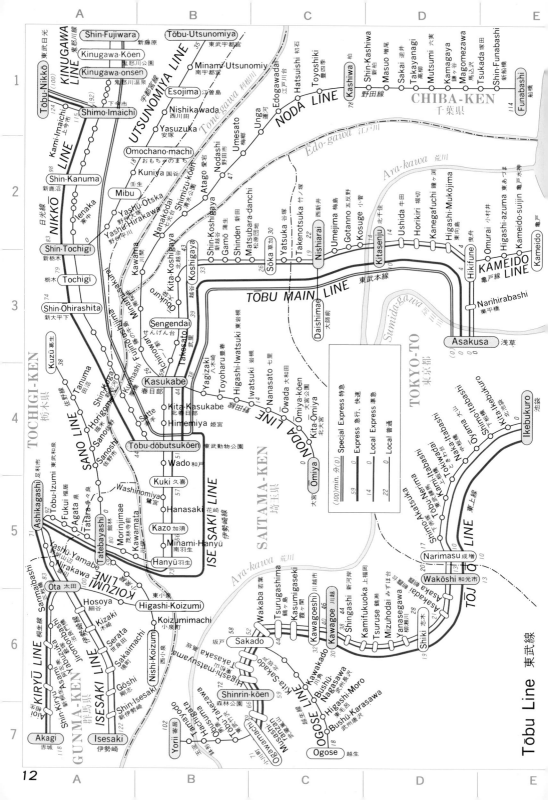

Tōbu Line 東武線

12

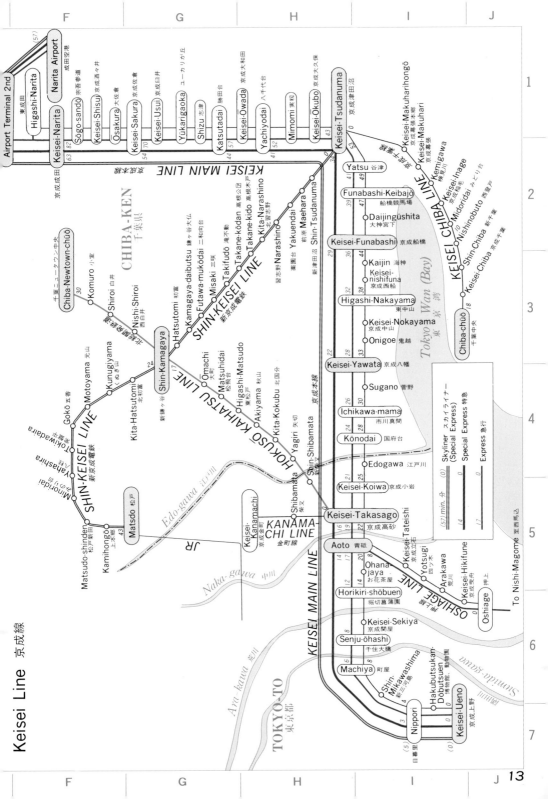

Keisei Line 京成線

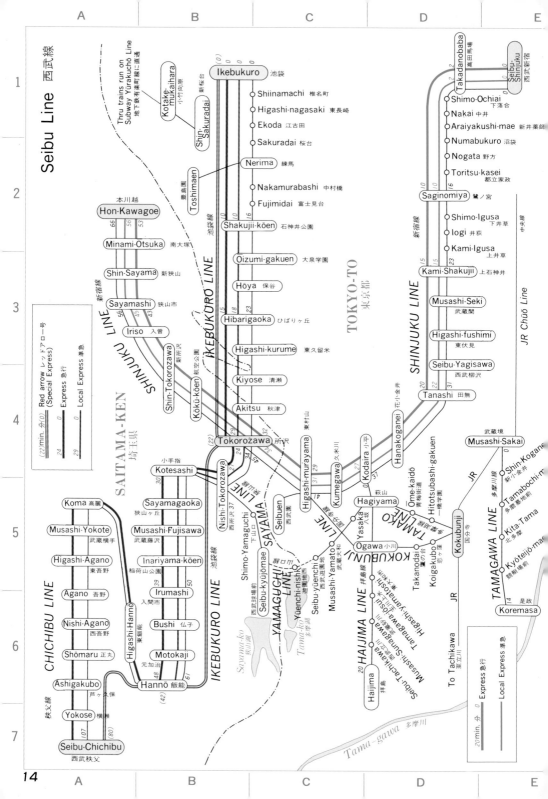

Seibu Line 西武線

Thru trains run on
Subway Yūrakuchō Line
地下鉄有楽町線に直通

Kotake-
mukaihara 小竹向原
Shin-Sakuradai 新桜台
Toshimaen 豊島園

Ikebukuro 池袋 (0)
Shiinamachi 椎名町
Higashi-nagasaki 東長崎
Ekoda 江古田
Sakuradai 桜台
Nerima 練馬
Nakamurabashi 中村橋
Fujimidai 富士見台
Shakujii-kōen 石神井公園
Oizumi-gakuen 大泉学園
Hōya 保谷
Hibarigaoka ひばりヶ丘
Higashi-kurume 東久留米
Kiyose 清瀬
Akitsu 秋津

Hon-Kawagoe 本川越 66 56 53
Minami-Otsuka 南大塚
Shin-Sayama 新狭山
Sayamashi 狭山市 56 45 43
Iriso 入曽
Shin-Tokorozawa 新所沢
Kōkū-kōen 航空公園
Tokorozawa 所沢 (22)

Takadanobaba 高田馬場 2
Seibu-Shinjuku 西武新宿
Shimo-Ochiai 下落合
Nakai 中井
Araiyakushi-mae 新井薬師前
Numabukuro 沼袋
Nogata 野方
Toritsu-kasei 都立家政
Saginomiya 鷺ノ宮
Shimo-Igusa 下井草
Iogi 井荻
Kami-Igusa 上井草
Kami-Shakujii 上石神井 15 15 23
Musashi-Seki 武蔵関
Higashi-fushimi 東伏見
Seibu-Yagisawa 西武柳沢
Tanashi 田無 20 22 31

IKEBUKURO LINE
SHINJUKU LINE
TOKYO-TO 東京都
JR Chūō Line
中央線

(22min. 分(0))
Red arrow レッドアロー号
(Special Express)
Express 急行
Local Express 準急
24 0
29 0

SAITAMA-KEN 埼玉県

Kotesashi 小手指 30
Sayamagaoka 狭山ヶ丘
Musashi-Fujisawa 武蔵藤沢
Inariyama-kōen 稲荷山公園
Irumashi 入間市 50
Bushi 仏子
Motokaji 元加治 61
Hannō 飯能 (42)

Koma 高麗
Musashi-Yokote 武蔵横手
Higashi-Agano 東吾野
Agano 吾野
Nishi-Agano 西吾野
Shōmaru 正丸
Ashigakubo 芦ヶ久保
Yokose 横瀬 (80)
Seibu-Chichibu 西武秩父 107

CHICHIBU LINE 秩父線
Higashi-Hannō 東飯能

Nishi-Tokorozawa 西所沢 37
Shimo-Yamaguchi 下山口
Seibu-kyūjōmae 西武球場前
Yūenchi-nishi 遊園地西
Seibu-yūenchi 西武遊園地
Tamako 多摩湖
Musashi-Yamato 武蔵大和
Yasaka 八坂

Higashi-murayama 東村山
Kumegawa 久米川
Yasaka 八坂
Ogawa 小川
Takanodai 鷹の台
Koigakubo 恋ヶ窪
Kokubunji 国分寺

Higashi-Yamatoshi 東大和市
Tamagawa-jōsui 玉川上水
Musashi-Sunagawa 武蔵砂川
Seibu-Tachikawa 西武立川
Haijima 拝島 20

SAYAMA LINE
YAMAGUCHI LINE
KOKUBUNJI LINE
TAMAKO LINE
HAIJIMA LINE 拝島線

Hagiyama 萩山
Ōme-kaidō 青梅街道
Hitotsubashi-gakuen 一橋学園
Kodaira 小平
Hanakoganei 花小金井

To Tachikawa 至立川
JR

Musashi-Sakai 武蔵境
Shin-Kogane 新小金井
Tamabochi-m 多磨墓地前
Kita-Tama 北多摩
Kyōteijō-mae 競艇場前
Koremasa 是政

TAMAGAWA LINE 多摩川線
JR

20min. 分 0 Express 急行
Local Express 準急

Sayama-ko 狭山湖
Tama-ko 多摩湖
Tama-gawa 多摩川

14

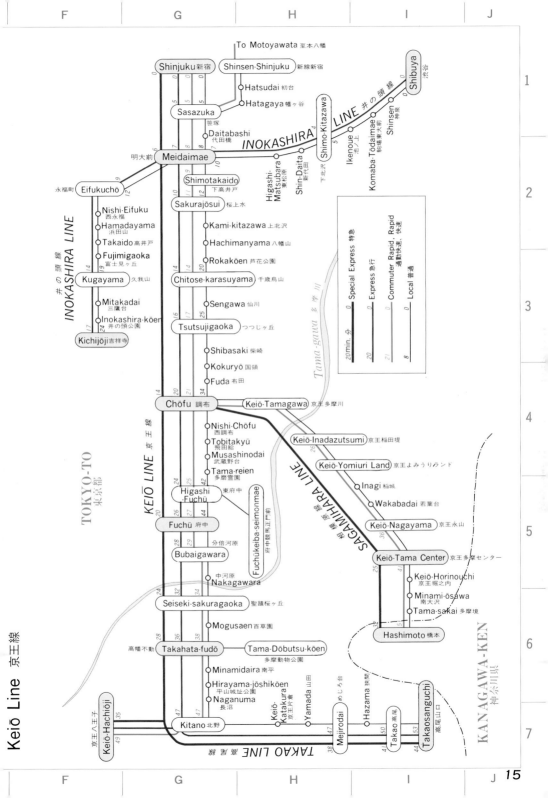

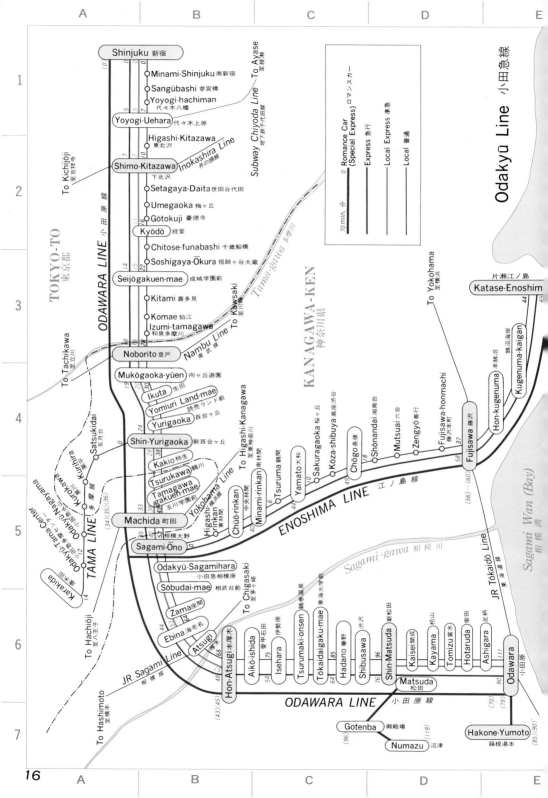

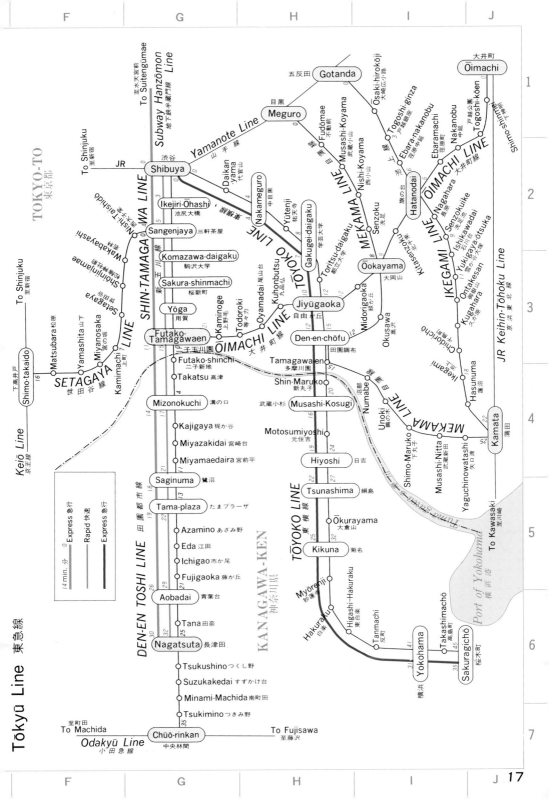

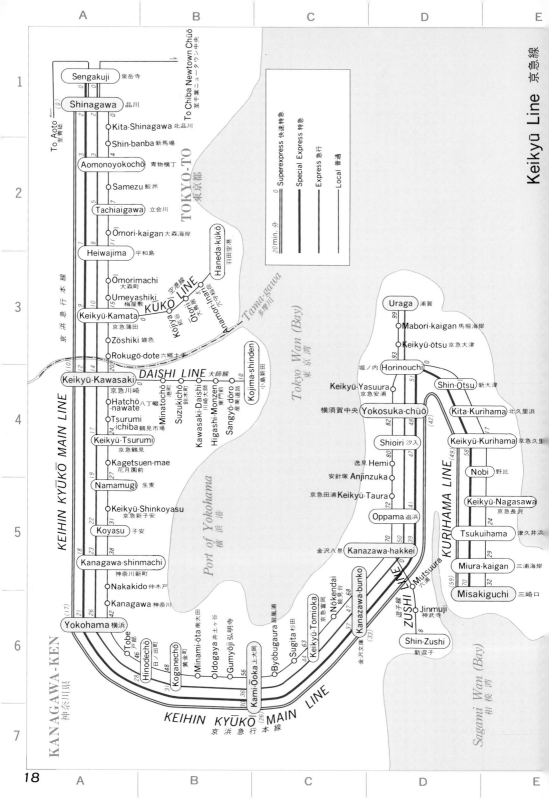

Keikyū Line 京急線

TOKYO-TO 東京都

Sengakuji 泉岳寺
Shinagawa 品川
Kita-Shinagawa 北品川
Shin-banba 新馬場
Aomonoyokochō 青物横丁
Samezu 鮫洲
Tachiaigawa 立会川
Ōmori-kaigan 大森海岸
Heiwajima 平和島
Ōmorimachi 大森町
Umeyashiki 梅屋敷
Keikyū-Kamata 京急蒲田
Zōshiki 雑色
Rokugō-dote 六郷土手
Keikyū-Kawasaki 京急川崎
Hatchō-nawate 八丁畷
Tsurumi-ichiba 鶴見市場
Keikyū-Tsurumi 京急鶴見
Kagetsuen-mae 花月園前
Namamugi 生麦
Keikyū-Shinkoyasu 京急新子安
Koyasu 子安
Kanagawa-shinmachi 神奈川新町
Nakakido 仲木戸
Kanagawa 神奈川
Yokohama 横浜
Tobe 戸部
Hinodechō 日ノ出町
Koganechō 黄金町
Minami-ōta 南太田
Idogaya 井土ケ谷
Gumyōji 弘明寺
Kami-Ōoka 上大岡

To Aoto 至青砥
To Chiba Newtown Chūō 至千葉ニュータウン中央

KUKO LINE 空港線
Kojiya 糀谷
Ōtorii 大鳥居
Anamori-Inari 穴守稲荷
Haneda-kūkō 羽田空港

Minatochō 港町
Suzukichō 鈴木町
Kawasaki-Daishi 川崎大師
Higashi-Monzen 東門前
Sangyō-dōro 産業道路
Kojima-shinden 小島新田

DAISHI LINE 大師線

Tama-gawa 多摩川

Tokyo Wan (Bay) 東京湾

KEIHIN KYŪKŌ MAIN LINE 京浜急行本線

Port of Yokohama 横浜港

KANAGAWA-KEN 神奈川県

KEIHIN KYŪKŌ MAIN LINE 京浜急行本線

Byōbugaura 屏風浦
Sugita 杉田
Keikyū-Tomioka 京急富岡
Nōkendai 能見台
Kanazawa-bunko 金沢文庫
Shin-Zushi 新逗子

Mutsuura 六浦
Jinmuji 神武寺
ZUSHI LINE 逗子線

Uraga 浦賀
Mabori-kaigan 馬堀海岸
Keikyū-ōtsu 京急大津
Horinouchi 堀ノ内
Keikyū-Yasuura 京急安浦
Yokosuka-chūō 横須賀中央
Shioiri 汐入
Hemi 逸見
Anjinzuka 安針塚
Keikyū-Taura 京急田浦
Oppama 追浜
Kanazawa-hakkei 金沢八景

Shin-Ōtsu 新大津
Kita-Kurihama 北久里浜
Keikyū-Kurihama 京急久里
Nobi 野比
Keikyū-Nagasawa 京急長沢
Tsukuihama 津久井浜
Miura-kaigan 三浦海岸
Misakiguchi 三崎口

KURIHAMA LINE 久里浜線

Sagami Wan (Bay) 相模湾

Superexpress 快速特急
Special Express 特急
Express 急行
Local 普通
20 min. 分

18

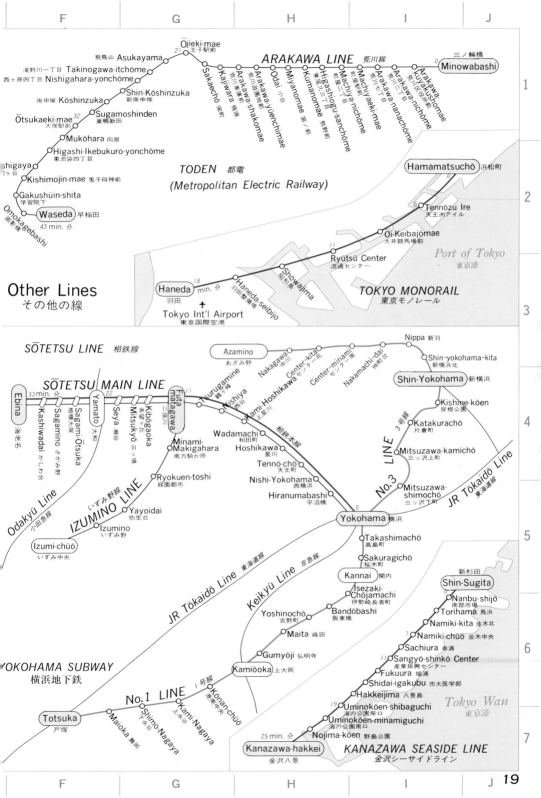

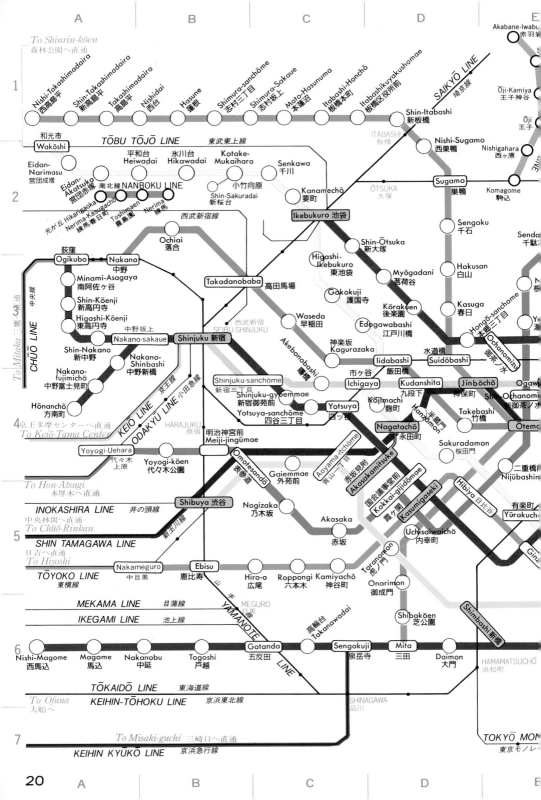

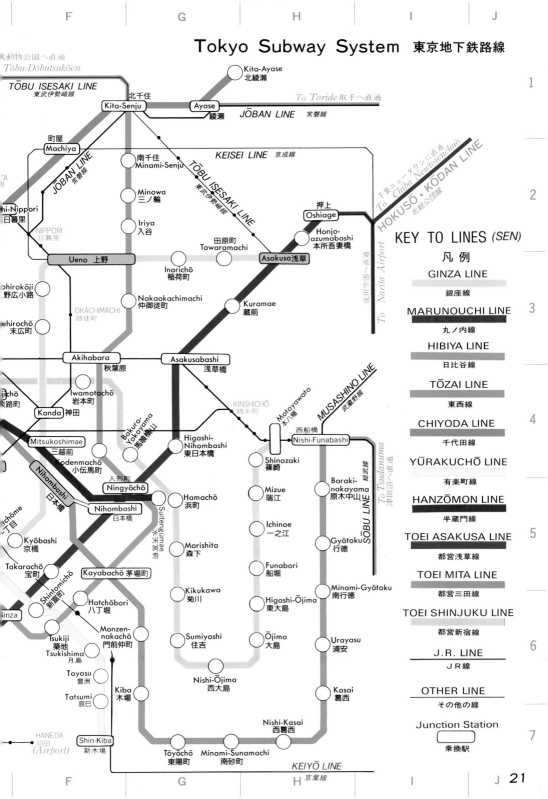

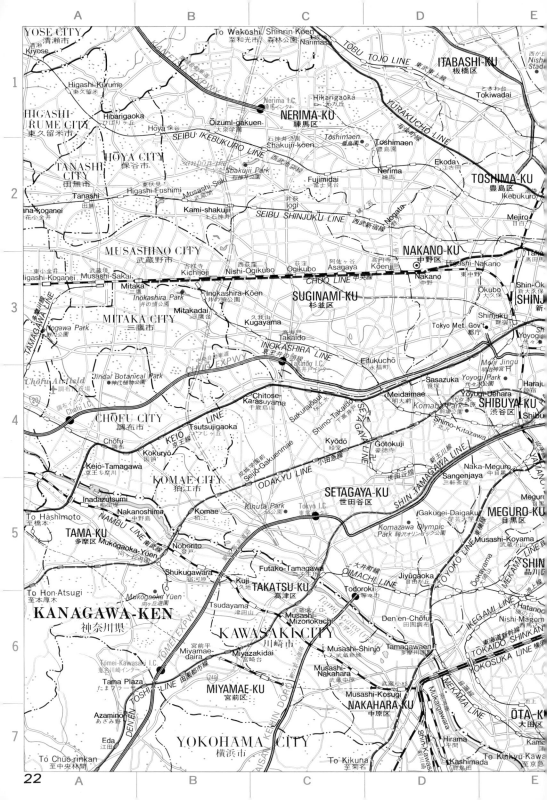

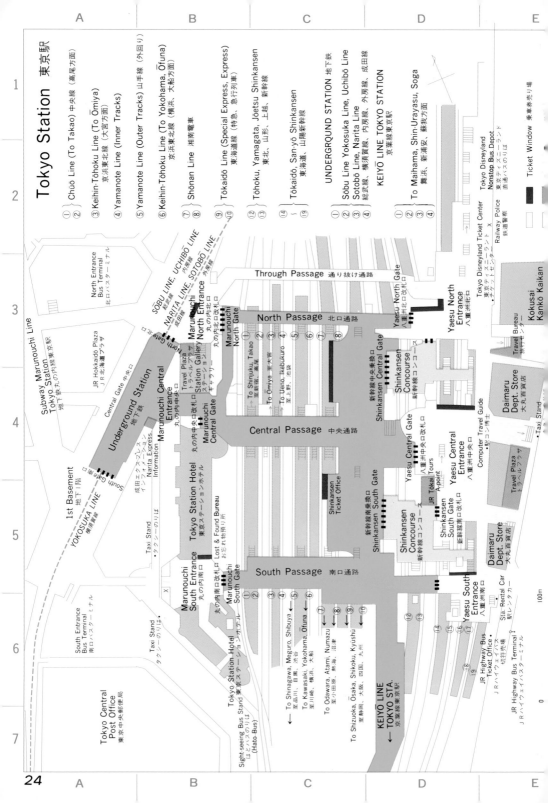

Tokyo Station 東京駅

① Chūō Line (To Takao) 中央線 (高尾方面)
②
③ Keihin-Tōhoku Line (To Ōmiya) 京浜東北線 (大宮方面)
④ Yamanote Line (Inner Tracks) 山手線 (内回り)
⑤ Yamanote Line (Outer Tracks) 山手線 (外回り) 山手線 (横浜、大船方面)
⑥ Keihin-Tōhoku Line (To Yokohama, Ōfuna) 京浜東北線 (横浜、大船方面)
⑦ Shōnan Line 湘南電車
⑧
⑨ Tōkaidō Line (Special Express, Express) 東海道線 (特急、急行列車)
⑩
⑫ Tōhoku, Yamagata, Jōetsu Shinkansen 東北、山形、上越、新幹線
⑬
⑭ Tōkaidō, San-yō Shinkansen 東海道、山陽新幹線
| ⑲

UNDERGROUND STATION 地下鉄
① Sōbu Line Yokosuka Line, Uchibō Line 総武線 横須賀線、内房線
② Sotobo Line, Narita Line 総武線、横須賀線、外房線、成田線
③
KEIYŌ LINE TOKYO STATION 京葉線東京駅
① To Maihama, Shin-Urayasu, Soga 舞浜、新浦安、蘇我方面
②
③
④

Tokyo Disneyland Ticket Center 東京ディズニーランド チケットセンター
Railway Police 鉄道警察
Ticket Window 乗車券売り場 ■
東車売り場 □

SŌBU LINE, UCHIBŌ LINE 総武線 内房線
NARITA LINE, SOTOBO LINE 成田線 外房線
YOKOSUKA LINE 横須賀線

Through Passage 通り抜け通路

North Passage 北口通路
Central Passage 中央通路
South Passage 南口通路

Marunouchi North Entrance 丸の内北口
Marunouchi North Gate 丸の内北口改札
Marunouchi Central Entrance 丸の内中央口
Marunouchi Central Gate 丸の内中央口改札
Marunouchi South Entrance 丸の内南口
Marunouchi South Gate 丸の内南口改札

Yaesu North Gate 八重洲北口改札
Yaesu North Entrance 八重洲北口
Yaesu Central Gate 八重洲中央口改札
Yaesu Central Entrance 八重洲中央口
Yaesu South Gate 八重洲南口改札
Yaesu South Entrance 八重洲南口

Shinkansen Central Gate 新幹線中央乗換口
Shinkansen Concourse 新幹線コンコース
Shinkansen South Gate 新幹線乗換口
Shinkansen Ticket Office 新幹線のりば

North Entrance Bus Terminal 北口バスターミナル
JR Hokkaido Plaza JR北海道プラザ
Subway Marunouchi Line Tokyo Station 地下鉄丸の内線東京駅
Underground Station 地下鉄
North Gate 北口
Central Gate 中央口
South Gate 南口

Narita Express 成田エクスプレス インフォメーション
Travel Plaza トラベルプラザ
Station Gallery ステーションギャラリー
Information 丸の内案内所
Tokyo Station Hotel 東京ステーションホテル
Lost & Found Bureau お忘れ物預り所
Tokyo Station Hotel 東京ステーションホテル

Computer Travel Guide 駅コンパス
Travel Plaza トラベルプラザ
Travel Bureau 旅行センター
JR Tōkai Tours A-point
JR Tokai Tours

Kokusai Kankō Kaikan
Daimaru Dept. Store 大丸百貨店
Taxi Stand タクシーのりば
Sta. Rental Car 駅レンタカー
Daimaru Dept. Store 大丸百貨店

1st Basement 地下1階
Taxi Stand タクシーのりば

Marunouchi Line
South Entrance Bus Terminal 南口バスターミナル
Taxi Stand タクシーのりば
Tokyo Central Post Office 東京中央郵便局

Sight-seeing Bus Stand はとバスのりば (Hato Bus) はとバスのりば

To Shinagawa, Meguro, Shibuya 至品川、目黒、渋谷
To Kawasaki, Yokohama, Ōfuna 至川崎、横浜、大船
To Odawara, Atami, Numazu 至小田原、熱海、沼津
To Shizuoka, Osaka, Shikoku, Kyushu 至静岡、大阪、四国、九州

KEIYŌ LINE ← TOKYO STA. 京葉線東京駅

JR Highway Bus Ticket Office JRハイウェイバス 切符売り場
JR Highway Bus Terminal JRハイウェイバスターミナル

Tokyo Disneyland Nonstop Bus Depot 東京ディズニーランド 直通バスのりば

100m
0

24

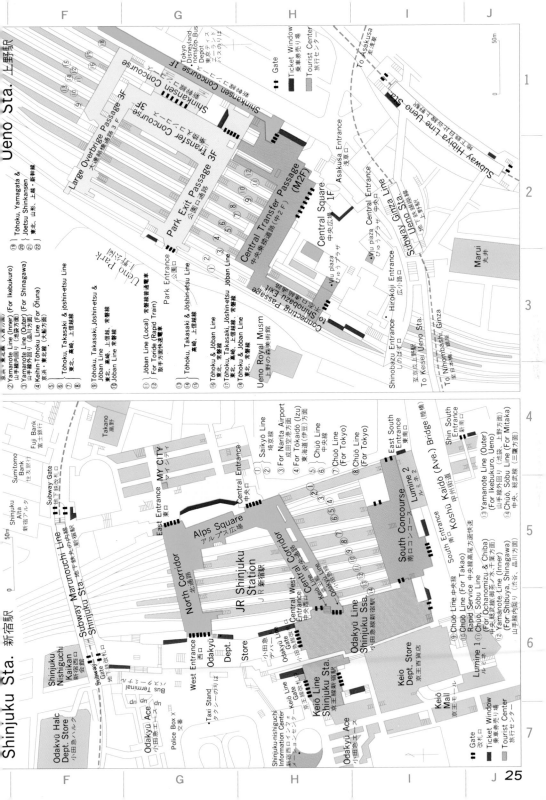

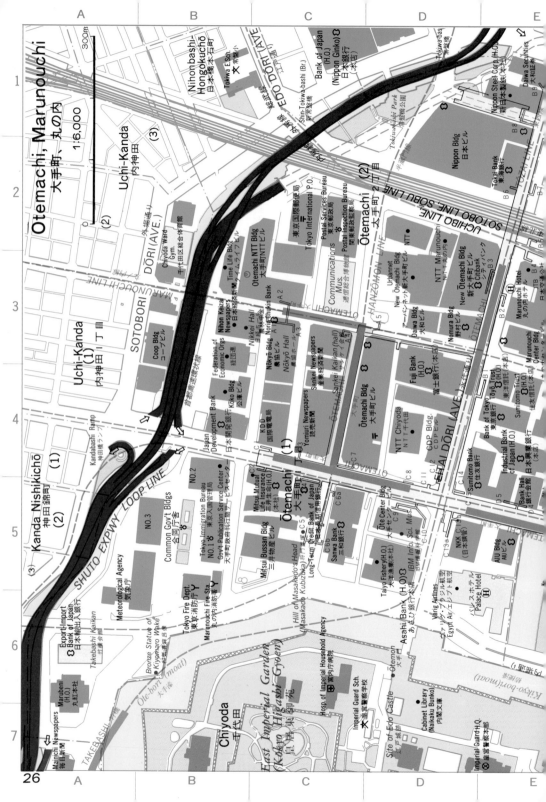

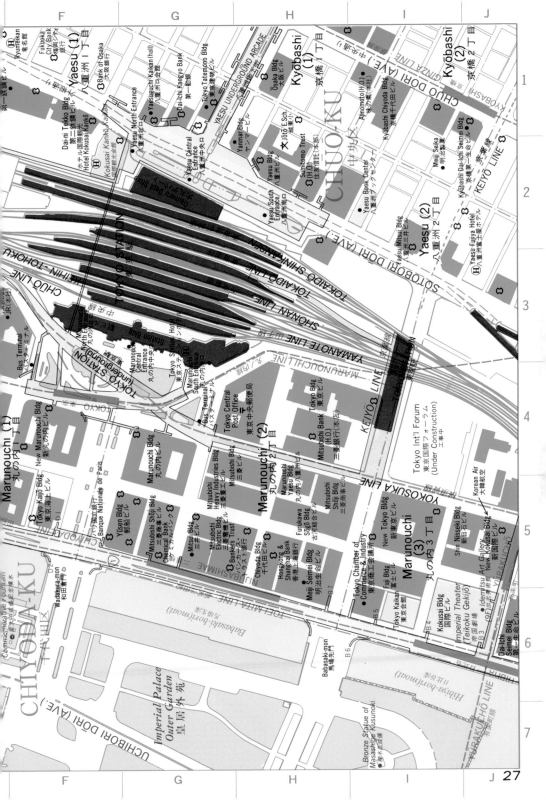

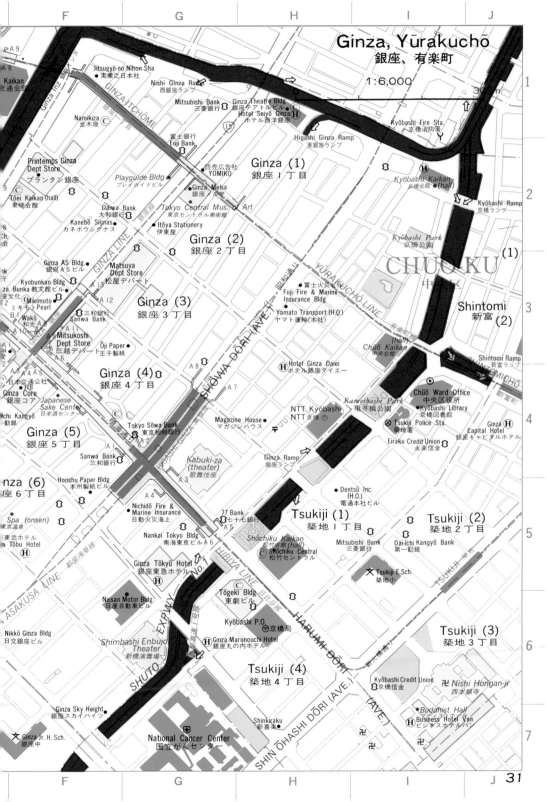

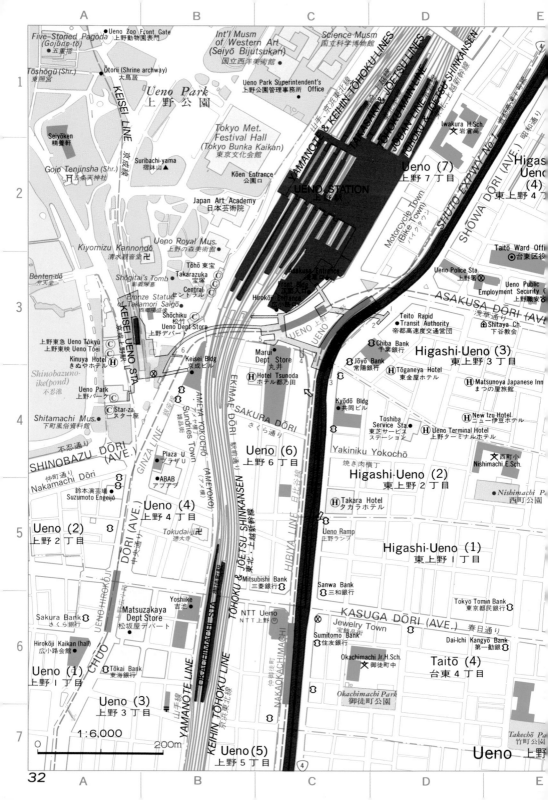

Akasakamitsuke 赤坂見附

Shimizudani Park 清水谷公園

Nihon Toshi Center 日本都市センター

Nihon Toshi Center Hall 日本都市センターホール

Zenkyōren Bldg 全共連ビル

Hotel New Ōtani ホテルニューオータニ

Kōjimachi Jr.H.Sch. 麹町中

Kioichō 紀尾井町

Japan Junior Chamber 日本青年会議所

SupremeCourt 最高裁判所

Guest House 旧館

Hotel New Ōtani Tower ホテルニューオータニタワー

Akasaka Prince Hotel 赤坂プリンスホテル

Sabō-kaikan Hall 砂防会館ホール

Sabō Kaikan 砂防会館

Benkei-bashi 弁慶橋

Tower 新館

Metropolitan District Hall (To-do-fu-ken Kaikan) 都道府県会館

IBM

Towns & Villages Kaikan 全国町村会館

Liberal-Democratic Party 自由民主党本部

Akasaka-mitsuke 赤坂見附 NAGATACHO 永田町

Nagatachō E.Sch. 永田町小

Moto-Akasaka 元赤坂

Suntory Mus. of Art サントリー美術館

衆議院議長公邸 Official Residence of the Speaker of the House of Representatives

参議院議長公邸 Official Residence of the President of the House of Councillors

(1)

Kajima Bldg 鹿島ビル

AIU Akasaka Bldg AIU赤坂ビル

Akasaka Tokyū Hotel 赤坂東急ホテル

(2)

Belle Vie Akasaka ベルビー赤坂

Akasaka Center Bldg 赤坂センタービル

Fuji Bank 富士

Emb. of Mexico メキシコ大使館

Members' Office House of Councillors 参議院議員会館

Toyokawa Inari 豊川稲荷

Akasaka-fudōson 赤坂不動尊

Sannō Grand Bldg 山王グランドビル

Nagatachō 永田町

Toraya 虎屋

Akasaka (4) 赤坂

(3)

Hibiya H. Sch. 日比谷高校

1 : 8,000

Akasaka Police Sta. 赤坂署

Sumitomo Seimei Akasaka Bldg 住友生命赤坂ビル

Hie Jinja (shrine) 日枝神社

200 m

Kasumigaseki 霞ヶ関

1 : 8,000

200 m

Tokyo Met. Police Dept.(H.Q) (Keishi-chō) 警視庁

Japan Barrister Assoc. 法曹会館

Iwaidabashi 祝田橋

Ministry of Construction 建設省

Nat'l Police Agency 警察庁

Ministry of Justice 法務署

Ministry of Transport 運輸省

Ministry of Home Affairs 自治省

Maritime Safety Agency 海上保安庁

Fire Defense Agency 消防庁

Tokyo High Court 東京高等裁判所

National Diet Building (Kokkai Gijidō) 国会議事堂

Nat'l Personnel Authority 人事院

Tokyo District Court 東京地方裁判所

Kasumigaseki Ramp 霞ヶ関ランプ

Ministry of Foreign Affairs 外務省

Public Prosecutor's Office 検察庁

Hibiya Park 日比谷公園

Science & Technology Agency 科学技術庁

Ministry of Agriculture, Forestry & Fisheries 農林水産省

Diet Press Center 国会記者会館

Kasumigaseki Ramp 霞ヶ関ランプ

Ministry of Health & Welfare 厚生省

Ministry of Labor 労働省

Prime Minister's Office 総理府

合同庁舎 No.4 Common Gov't Bldg

Environment Agency 環境庁

Nat'l Land Agency 国土庁

Kasumigaseki (1) 霞ヶ関

Okinawa Develop. Agency 沖縄開発庁

Hokkaido Develop. Agency 北海道開発庁

(2)

Publication Service Center 政府刊行物サービスセンター

Hibiya-Kōen 日比谷公園

New Kasumigaseki Bldg 新霞ヶ関ビル

Ministry of Finance 大蔵省

Tokyo Family Court 東京家裁

会計検査院 Board of Audit

Ministry of Int'l Trade & Industry 通商産業省

都立日比谷図書館 Met. Hibiya Library

Hibiya Public Hall 日比谷公会堂

Patent Office 特許庁

Kasumigaseki Bldg 霞が関ビル

Ministry of Education 文部省

Ministry of Posts & Telecommunications 郵政省

Nippon Press Center 日本プレスセンター

Jiji Press 時事通信社

Nat'l Education Center 国立教育会館

Fukoku Mutual Life Insurance 富国生命

Tokyo Club Bldg 東京倶楽部ビル

Toranomon Hall 虎ノ門ホール

Tokyo Expwy Public Corp. 首都高速道路公団

Iino Bldg 飯野ビル

Iino Hall イイノホール

日比谷国際ビル Hibiya Kokusai Bldg

Hibiya City 日比谷シティ

Tōtō 東陶

Diamond Sha ダイヤモンド社

35

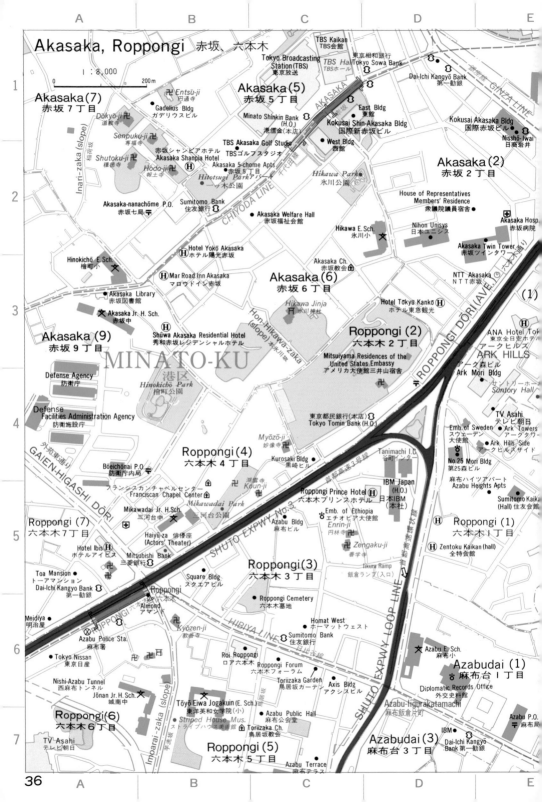

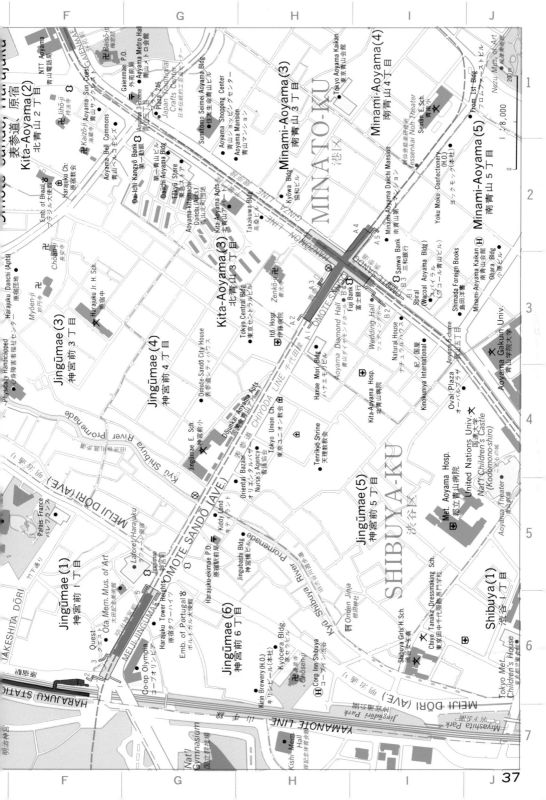

Shibuya, Harajuku, Aoyama

表参道, 原宿
Kita-Aoyama(2)
北青山 2 丁目

NTT Aoyama
青山電話局

Galenmae P.O.
外苑前局

Jihō-ji
持法寺

Aoyama 3-chome
青山三丁目

Plaza 246

Aoyama Sun-Crest
青山サンクレスト

Japan Traditional
Crafts Center
日本伝統工芸館

Sumitomo Seimei Aoyama3 Bldg
住友生命青山3ビル

Tokyo Aoyama Kaikan
東京青山会館

Minami-Aoyama(4)
南青山 4 丁目

From 1st Bldg
フロンティアビル

Nezu Mus. of Art
根津美術館

MINATO-KU
港区

Minami-Aoyama(5)
南青山 5 丁目

1 : 8,000

Seinan E. Sch.
西南小

Tessenkai Noh Theater

Minami-Aoyama(3)
南青山 3 丁目

Aoyama Shopping Center
青山ショッピングセンター

Aoyama Mansion
青山マンション

Daiichi Aoyama Mansion
第一青山マンション

Kaizō-ji
海蔵寺

Aoyama Bell Commons
青山ベルコモンズ

Harajuku Ch:
原宿教会

Dai-Ichi Kangyō Bank
第一勧銀

Tokyu Store
東急ストア

Daiichi Aoyama Bldg
第一青山ビル

Kyōwa Bldg
協和ビル

Minami-Aoyama Daiichi Mansion
南青山第一マンション

Yoku Moku Confectionery
ヨックモック(本社)

Emb. of Brazil
ブラジル大使館

Chōan-ji
長安寺

Aoyama-Kitamachi
Danchi (Apts.)
青山北町団地

Kita-Aoyama Apts.
北青山アパート

Takakuwa Bldg
高桑ビル

Minami-Aoyama Kaikan
南青山会館

Ohara Bldg
小原ビル

Myōen-ji
妙円寺

Harajuku Jr. H. Sch.
原宿中

Sanwa Bank
三和銀行

Shimada Foreign Books
島田洋書

Wacoal Aoyama Bldg
(ワコール青山ビル)

Jingūmae (3)
神宮前 3 丁目

Jingūmae (4)
神宮前 4 丁目

Kita-Aoyama (3)
北青山 3 丁目

Tokyo Central Bldg
東京セントラルビル

Itō Hosp.
伊藤病院

Zenkō-ji
善光寺

Fuji Bank
富士銀行

Spiral

Aoyama Diamond Hall
青山ダイヤモンドホール

Natural House
ナチュラルハウス

Aoyama 5-chome
青山五丁目

Aoyama Gakuin Univ.
青山学院大学

Physically Handicapped
身体障害者福祉センター

Harajuku Danchi (Apts)
原宿団地

Jingūmae E. Sch.
神宮前小

Dōjunkai Aoyama Apts
同潤会青山アパート

Tokyo Union Ch.
東京ユニオン教会

Wedding Hall
ウエディングホール

Hanae Mori Bldg
ハナエモリビル

Kita-Aoyama Hosp.
北青山病院

Kinokuniya International

Oval Plaza
オーバルプラザ

Kyū Shibuya River Promenade

Meiji Dōri (Ave.)

Harajuku

Jingūmae (5)
神宮前 5 丁目

Tenrikyō Shrine
天理教教会

Omote-Sandō City House
表参道シティハウス

Oriental Bazaar
オリエンタルバザール

Kiddy Land
キデイランド

Nurse's Agency
看護協会

Onden Jinja
穏田神社

Met. Aoyama Hosp.
都立青山病院

United Nations Univ.
国連大学

Nat'l Children's Castle
(Kodomo-shiro)
こどもの城

SHIBUYA-KU
渋谷区

Aoyama Theater
青山劇場

Palais France
パレフランス

Jingūmae (1)
神宮前 1 丁目

Ōta Mem. Mus. of Art
太田記念美術館

Laforet/Harajuku
ラフォーレ原宿

Jingūmae
神宮前

Harajuku Tower Heights
原宿タワーハイツ

Harajuku-ekimae P.O.
原宿駅前局

Omote Sandō (Ave.)

Jingūmae (6)
神宮前 6 丁目

Jingubashi Bldg
神宮橋ビル

Quest
クエスト

Co-op Olympia
コープオリンピア

Emb. of Portugal
ポルトガル大使館

Kyū Shibuya River Promenade

Kirin Brewery
キリンビール(本社)

Kyōcera Bldg
京セラビル(本社)

Chōsen-ji
長泉寺

Corp Inn Shibuya
コープイン渋谷

Shibuya (1)
渋谷 1 丁目

Shibuya Girls' H. Sch.
渋谷女子高

Chiyo Tanaka Dressmaking Sch.
東京中千代服飾専門学校

Tokyo Met. Children's House
東京都児童会館

Jakeshita Dōri

Harajuku Station

Nat'l Gymnasium
国立代々木競技場

Kishi Mem. Hall
岸記念体育館

Yamanote Line

Jingūdori Park
神宮通公園

Miyashita Park
宮下公園

Meiji Dōri (Ave.)

Chiyoda Line 千代田線

Ginza Line 銀座線

A 4

A 5

B 1

B 2

B 3

Shinjuku 新宿

Naruko Tenjinsha 成子天神社

Jōon-ji 浄音寺

Nishi-Shinjuku (8)
西新宿 8 丁目

ŌME KAIDO (AVE.) 青梅街道

Yamaguchi Bank 山口銀行

Hyōgo Bank 兵庫

Kashiwagi Bldg 柏木ビル

Shinjuku Health Centre 新宿保健所

Tokyo Language 東京外語専門学

Shōkō Chukin Ban 商工中金ビ

Yodobashi Daiichi E. Sch 淀橋一小

Yodobashi Daiichi Kindergarten 淀橋第一幼稚園

Nishi-Shinjuku (7)
西新宿 7 丁目

Kashiwagi Park 柏木公園

Tōhō 東邦銀

Daikan Plaza ダイカンプラ

Tenriism Central Shr 天理教中央教会

MARUNOUCHI LINE 丸ノ内線

Tokyo Cookery Academy 東京調理師専門学校

Star Hotel Tokyo スターホテル東京

Tōkyō Ba

Nishi-Shinjuku (6)
西新宿 6 丁目

Tokyo Medical College Hospital 東京医科大学病院

Rōsai Kaikan (hall) 労災会館

Yamagata Shiawase Bank 山形しあわせ銀行

Jōen-ji 常円寺

Jōsen-ji 常泉寺

Shinjuku Police Sta. 新宿署

Shōwa Shinki 昭和信金

Jōfu-ji 浄風寺

Tokyo Hilton Int'l 東京ヒルトンインターナショナル

Met. Bureau of Waterworks 都水道局(支) (Branch Office)

Shinjuku Nomura Bldg
新宿野村ビル (50Fl)
Free Observatory 無料展望ロビー (50Fl)
Nomura Hall 野村ホール (B1)

Yasuda Kasai-Kaijo Bldg (43Fl)
安田火災海上本社ビル
Togo Seiji Art Museum 東郷青児美術館 (42Fl)

Odakyū 小田急

Shinjuku Kokusai Bldg 新宿国際ビル

Waterworks Mus. 東京都水道記念館

KITA DŌRI (AVE.) 北通り

Sanwa Bank 三和銀行

A 18

B 18

Green Tower Bldg グリーンタワービル

Shinjuku Mitsui Bldg
新宿三井ビル (55Fl)
Observation Restaurant 展望レストラン (54〜55Fl)

Shinjuku L Tower 新宿Lタワー

Sumitomo Bank 住友銀行

A 17

Matsuoka Centr 松岡セントラル

Shinjuku Daiich Seimei Bldg 新宿第一生命ビル

Shinjuku Sumitomo Bldg
新宿住友ビル (52Fl)
Free Observatory 無料展望ロビー (51Fl)
Asahi Culture Center 朝日カルチャーセンター
Sumitomo Hall (B1) 住友ホール

Shinjuku Center Bldg
新宿センタービル (54Fl)
Free Observatory 無料展望台 (53Fl)

Asahi Mutual Life Insurance (H.O.) 朝日生命本社ビル

Asahi Seimei Hall 朝日生命ホール

Dai-Ichi Kangyō Bank 第一勧業

Subaru Bldg スバルビル

OD

Nishi-Shinjuku (1)
西新宿 1 丁目

Hotel Century Hyatt ホテルセンチュリーハイアット

TOCHŌ DŌRI (AVE.) 都庁通り

GIJIDŌ DŌRI (AVE.) 議事堂通り

HIGASHI DŌRI (AVE.)

CHŪO DŌRI (AVE.) 中央通り

West E

Kōgakuin Univ. 工学院大学

Meiji Seimei Bldg 明治生命ビル

Yasuda Seimei Bldg 安田生命ビル

Shinjuku Bldg 新宿ビル

Fuji Bank 富士銀行

Yasuda Seimei Hall 安田生命ホール

ODAKYŪ 小田急

Keio Plaza Hotel (47Fl) 京王プラザホテル

Shinjuku P.O. 新宿局

Plaza Dōri プラザ通り

Hokkaido Bank 北海道銀行

Nishi-Shinjuku (2)
西新宿 2 丁目

KŌEN DŌRI (AVE.)

Shinjuku Central Park 新宿中央公園

Met. Assembly Hall 都議会議事堂

Keio Plaza Hotel (South Tower) 京王プラザホテル南館

Kadoya Hotel かどやホテル

Yamanashi Chūō Bank 山梨中央銀行

Chūo Dōri (Ave.) 中央通り東洋信託

Highway Bus Terminal 高速バスターミナル

Yodobashi Camera ヨドバシカメラ

Mitsubish

Tōyō Trust

Metropolitan Government Office 東京都庁

Shinjuku NS Bldg (30Fl)
新宿NSビル

Shinjuku Monolith
新宿モノリス

NTT Yodobashi NTT淀橋

San'ei Bldg サンエービル

People's Finance Corp. 国民金融公庫

Industrial Bank of Japan 興銀

Sakuraya Camera カメラのさくらや

Doi Camera カメラのドイ

Meihō Bldg 明宝ビル

Shinjuku Sky Bldg 新宿スカイビル

KDD Bldg (32Fl)
KDDビル

Taihei Bldg 太平ビル

Sakura Bank さくら銀行

Kubo Blc 久保ビ

Fukutoku Bank 福徳銀行

KDD P.O. KDD内局

Tsunohazu-bashi (Br.) 角筈橋

MINAMI DŌRI (AVE.) 南通り

Tokyo Kaijo Bldg 東京海上ビル

KEIŌ LINE (NEW LINE)

Sakakibara Mem. 榊原記念病院

Hotel Sunr ホテルサン

Shinjuku Washington Hotel 新宿ワシントンホテル

KEIŌ LINE 京王線

Yoyogi 代々木

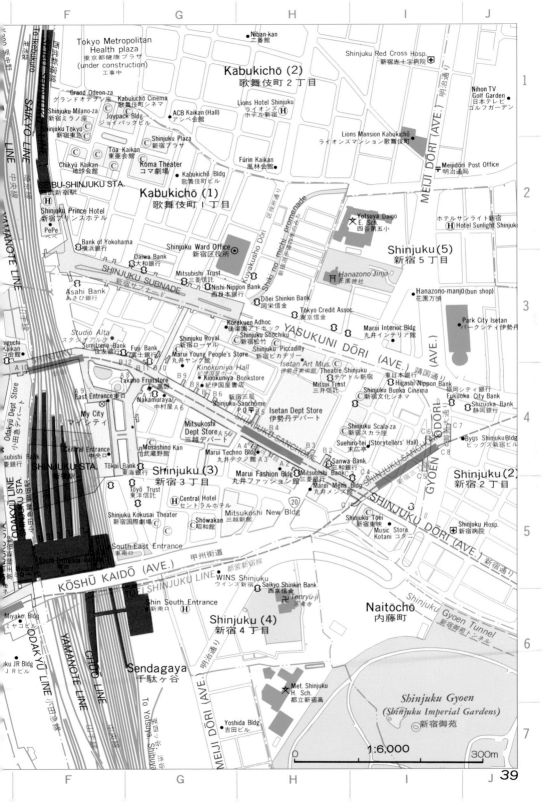

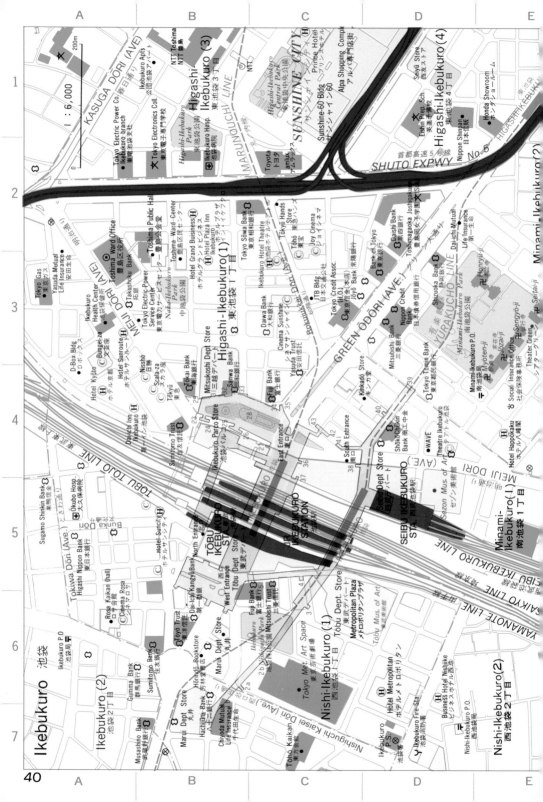

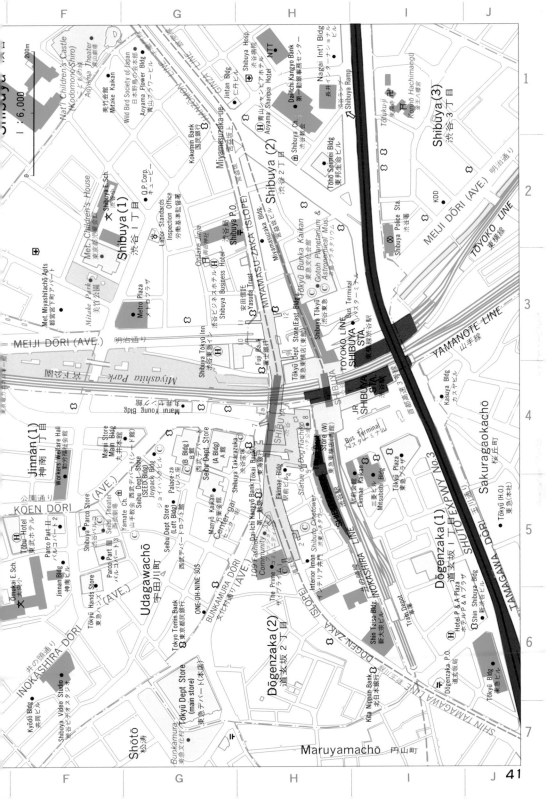

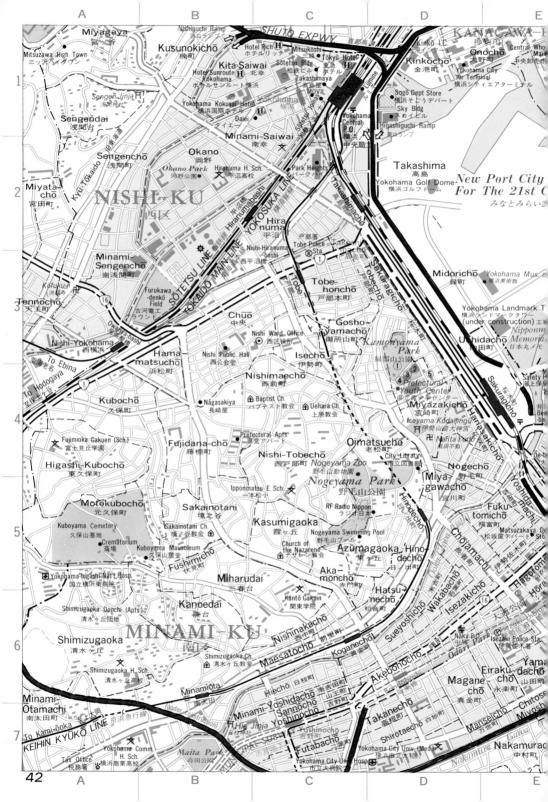

Central Yokohama
横浜中心部

① Bronze Statue of Naosuke Ii　井伊直弼像
② Prefectural Concert Hall　県立音楽堂
③ Prefectural Library　県立図書館
④ Science Museum　文化資料館
⑤ Kanagawa Youth Hostel　神奈川ユースホステル
⑥ Opening Port Mem. Hall　開港記念会館
⑦ Yokohama Archives of History　横浜開港資料館
⑧ Silk Museum　シルク博物館
⑨ Yokohama Doll Museum　横浜人形の家
⑩ Yokohama Marine Science Musm　横浜海洋科学博物館
⑪ Yamate Museum　山手資料館
⑫ Iwasaki Museum　岩崎博物館
⑬ Jiro Osaragi Mem. Museum　大仏次郎記念館
⑭ Kanagawa Mus. of Modern Literature　神奈川近代文学館

1 : 20,000

0   500 m

43

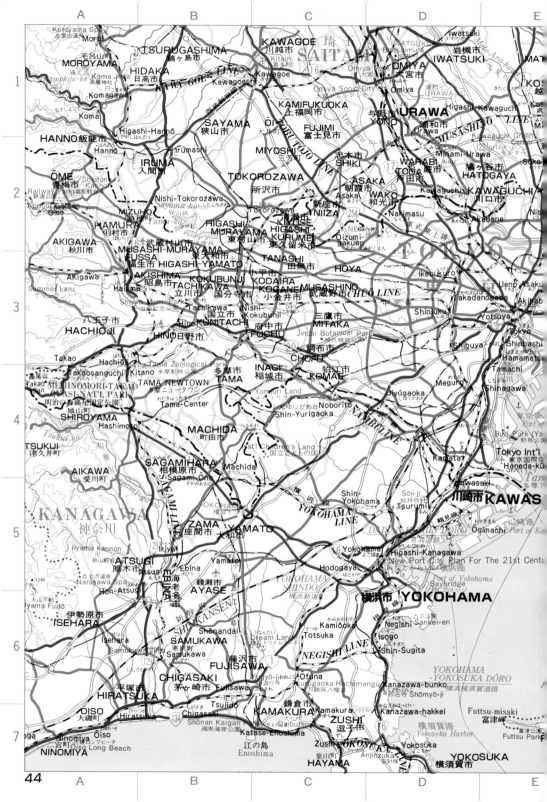

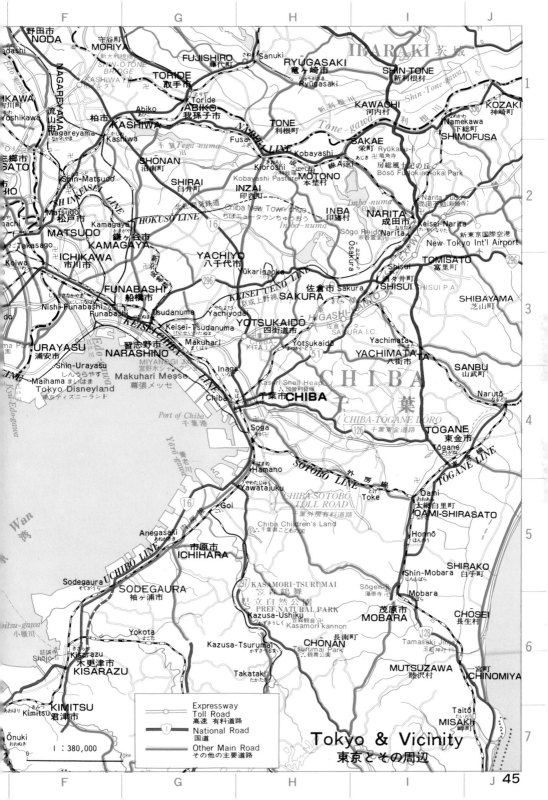

Tokyo & Vicinity
東京とその周辺

1 : 380,000

		Expressway
		Toll Road
		高速 有料道路
		National Road
		国道
		Other Main Road
		その他の主要道路

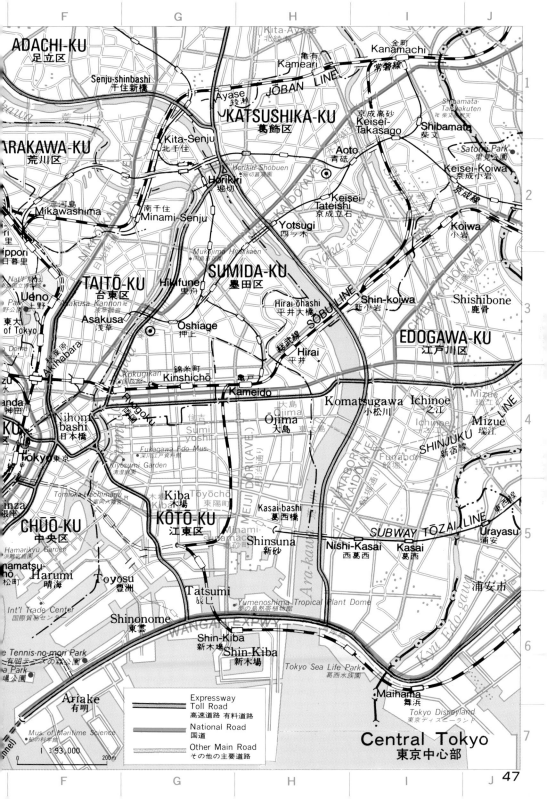

Central Tokyo
東京中心部

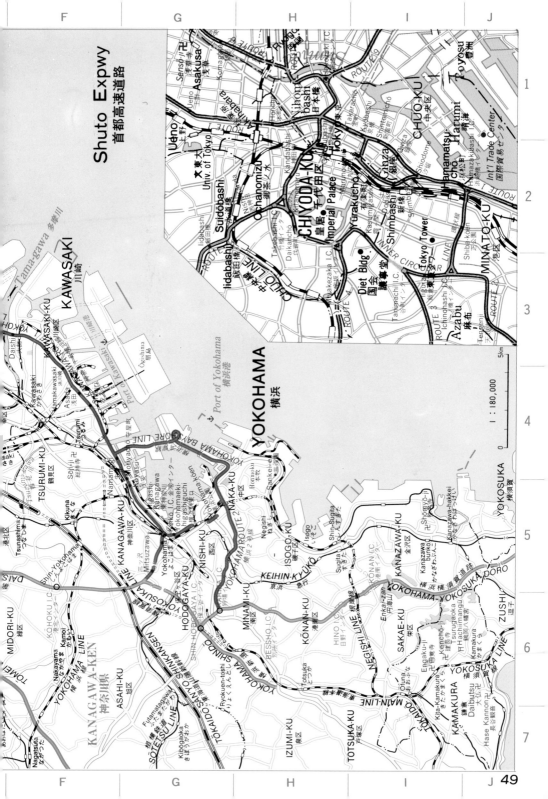

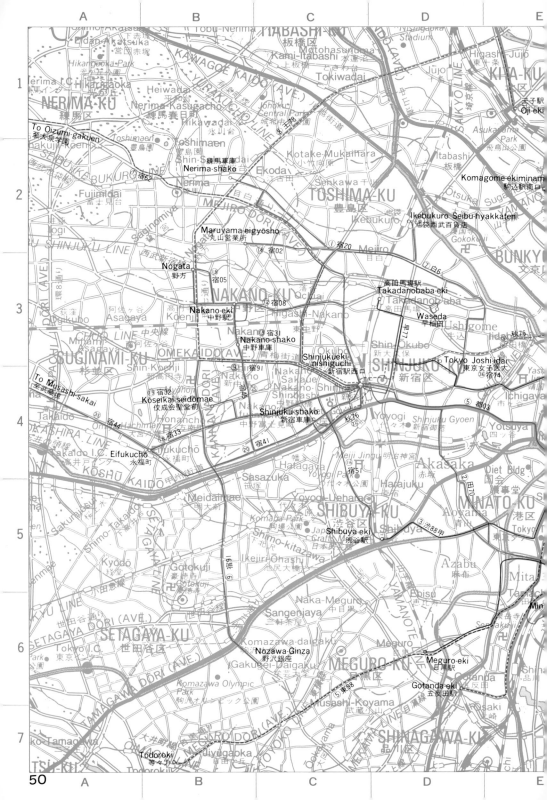

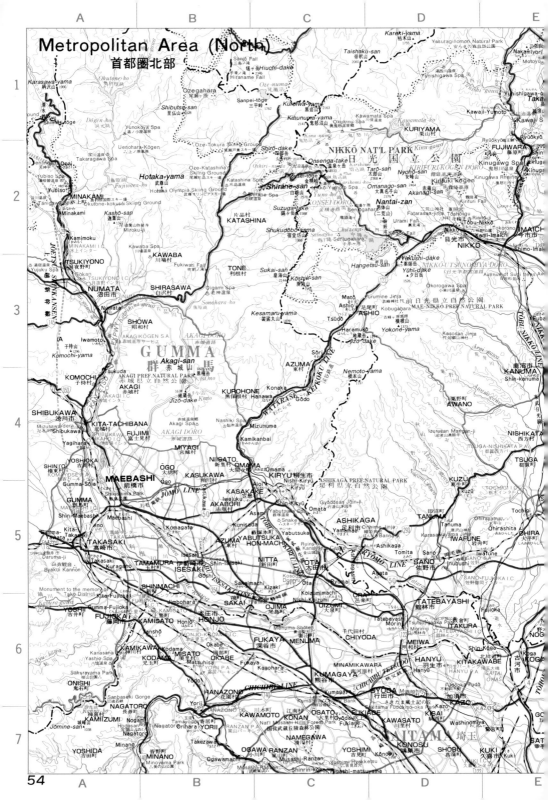

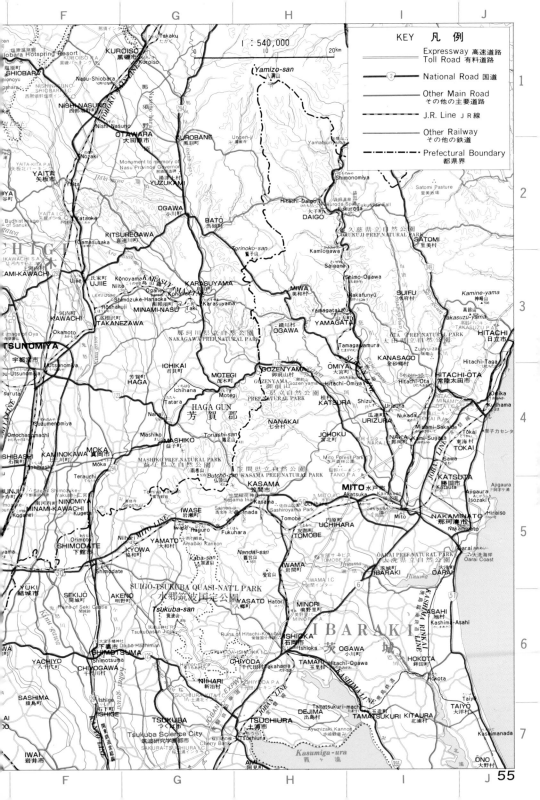

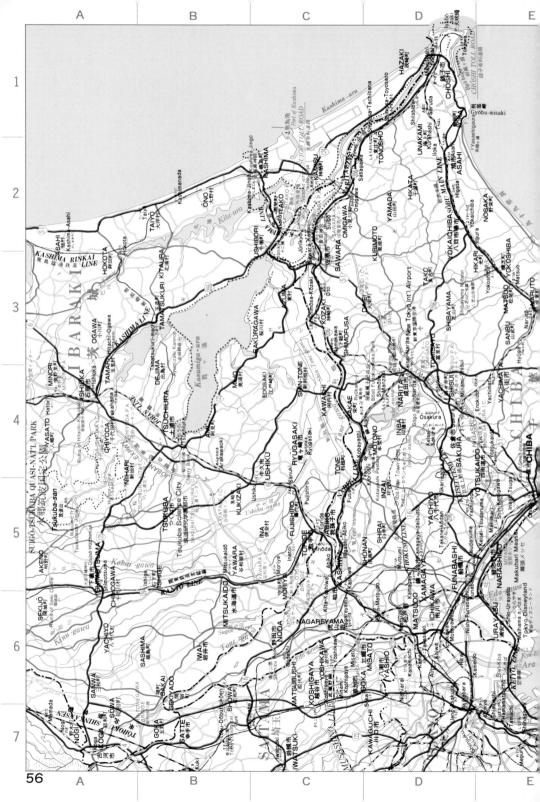

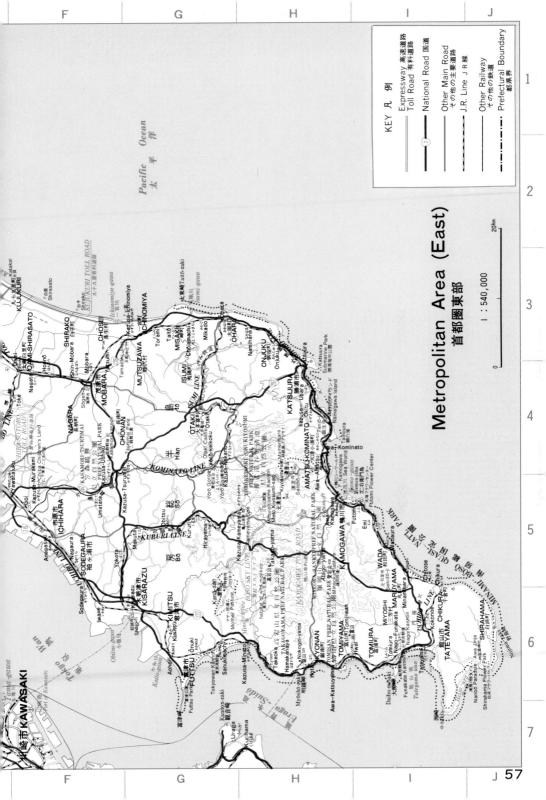

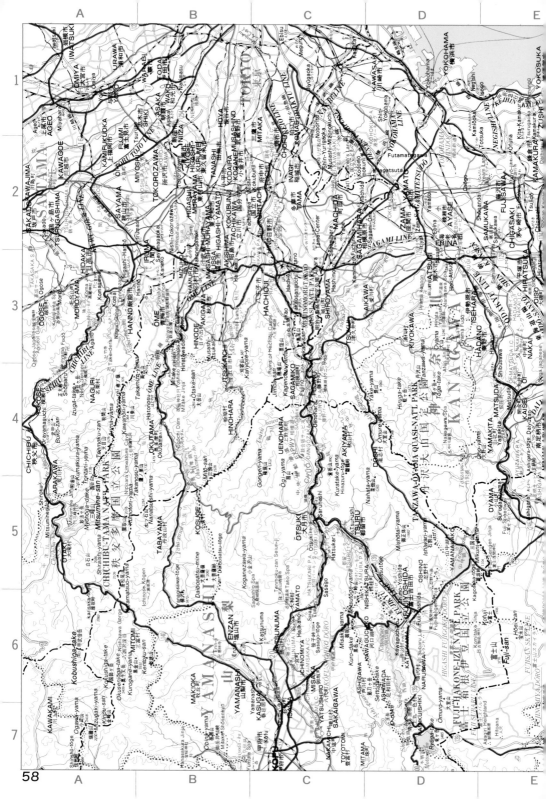
58

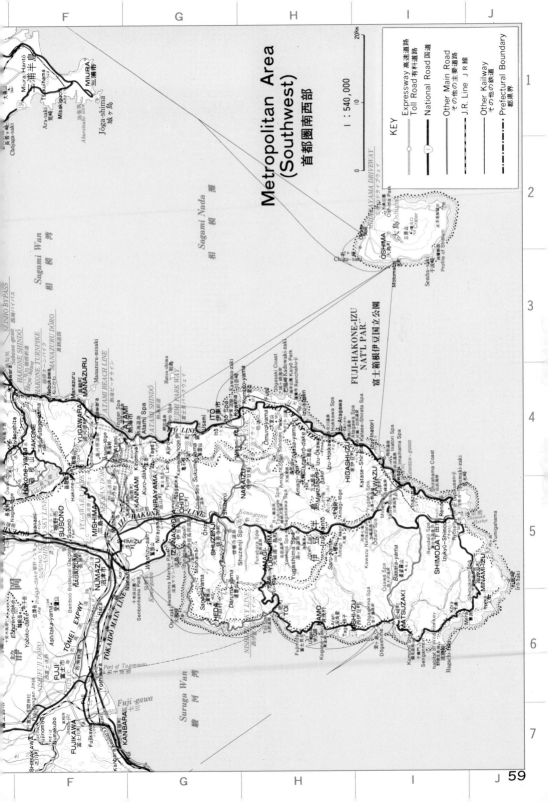

Metropolitan Area (Southwest)
首都圏南西部

1 : 540,000

Sagami Nada　相模灘

Sagami Wan　相模湾

Suruga Wan　駿河湾

FUJI-HAKONE-IZU NAT'L PARK
富士箱根伊豆国立公園

OSHIMA　大島

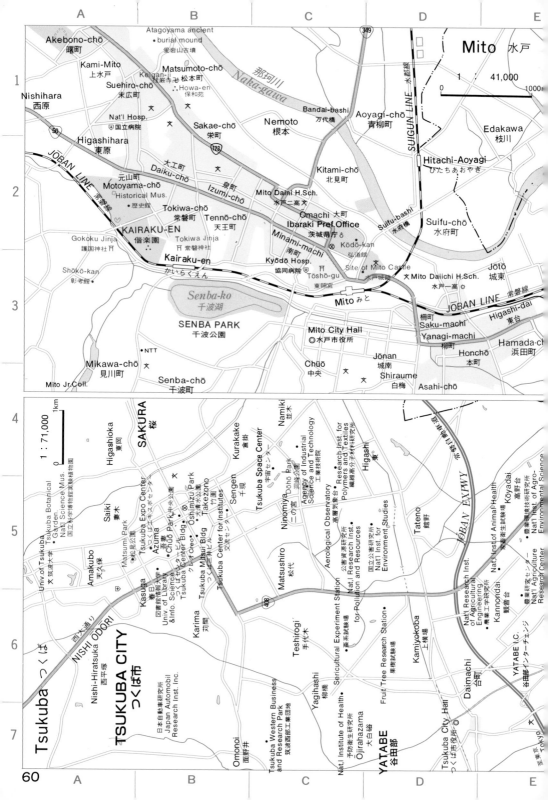

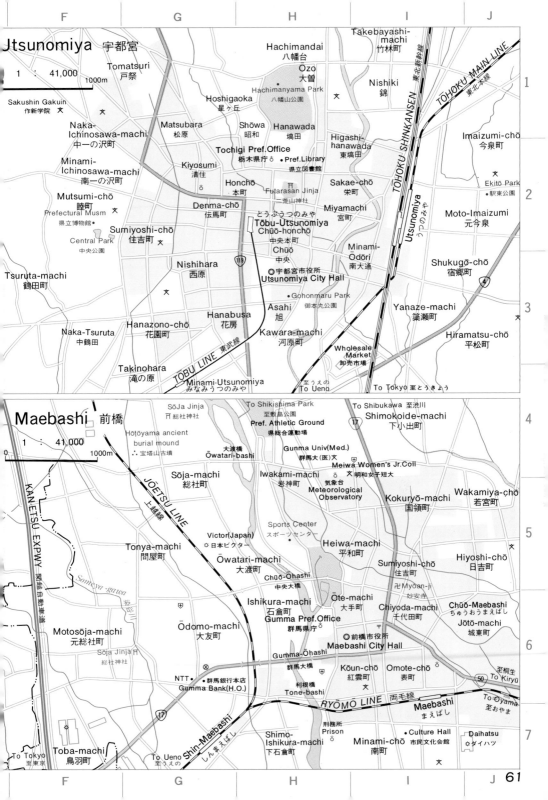

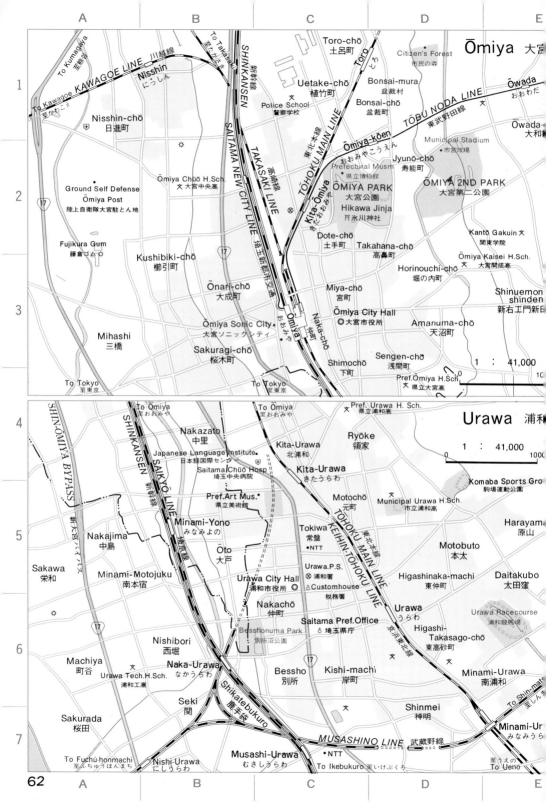

Ōmiya 大宮

Toro-chō
土呂町

To Kumagaya
至くまがや

To Takasaki
至たかさき

1

Citizen's Forest
市民の森

Nisshin
にっしん

川越線
KAWAGOE LINE

To Kawagoe
至かわごえ

SHINKANSEN
新幹線

Uetake-chō
植竹町

Bonsai-mura
盆栽村

Bonsai-chō
盆栽町

TŌBU NODA LINE
東武野田線

Ōwada
おおわだ

Nisshin-chō
日進町

Police School
警察学校

Ōwada-chō
大和田町

2

SAITAMA NEW CITY LINE

TAKASAKI LINE 高崎線

Ōmiya-kōen
おおみやこうえん

Municipal Stadium
市宮球場

Ground Self Defense
Ōmiya Post
陸上自衛隊大宮駐とん地

Ōmiya Chūō H.Sch.
大宮中央高

TŌHOKU MAIN LINE 東北本線

Kita-Ōmiya
きたおおみや

Prefectural Musm
県立博物館

Jyunō-chō
寿能町

ŌMIYA PARK
ŌMIYA 2ND PARK
大宮公園
大宮第二公園

Hikawa Jinja
氷川神社

Kantō Gakuin
関東学院

Fujikura Gum
藤倉ゴム

Kushibiki-chō
櫛引町

Ōmiya Kaisei H.Sch.
大宮開成高

Dote-chō
土手町

Takahana-chō
高鼻町

Horinouchi-chō
堀の内町

3

SAITAMA NEW CITY LINE 埼玉新都市交通

Miya-chō
宮町

Shinuemon
shinden
新右エ門新田

Mihashi
三橋

Ōnari-chō
大成町

Ōmiya Sonic City
大宮ソニックシティ

Ōmiya
おおみや

Naka-chō
仲町

Ōmiya City Hall
大宮市役所

Amanuma-chō
天沼町

Sakuragi-chō
桜木町

Shimochō
下町

Sengen-chō
浅間町

1 : 41,000

To Tokyo
至東京

To Tokyo
至東京

Pref.Ōmiya H.Sch.
県立大宮高

Urawa 浦和

4

SHIN-ŌMIYA BYPASS
新大宮バイパス

To Ōmiya
至おおみや

To Ōmiya
至おおみや

Pref. Urawa H. Sch.
県立浦和高

Nakazato
中里

SHINKANSEN
新幹線

Japanese Language Institute.
日本語国際センター

Saitama Chūō Hosp.
埼玉中央病院

Kita-Urawa
北浦和

Ryōke
領家

1 : 41,000

0   1000

SAIKYŌ LINE

Kita-Urawa
きたうらわ

Komaba Sports Gro
駒場運動公園

Pref.Art Mus.
県立美術館

Motochō
元町

Municipal Urawa H.Sch.
市立浦和高

5

Nakajima
中島

Minami-Yono
みなみよの

TŌHOKU MAIN LINE

Harayama
原山

Tokiwa
常盤

Motobuto
本太

Ōto
大戸

Urawa P.S.
浦和P.S.

KEIHIN-TŌHOKU LINE 京浜東北線

Sakawa
栄和

Minami-Motojuku
南本宿

Urawa City Hall
浦和市役所

Customhouse
税務署

Higashinaka-machi
東仲町

Daitakubo
太田窪

Nakachō
仲町

Urawa
うらわ

6

Bessho numa Park
別所沼公園

Saitama Pref.Office
埼玉県庁

Higashi-
Takasago-chō
東高砂町

Urawa Racecourse
浦和競馬場

Machiya
町谷

Nishibori
西堀

Naka-Urawa
なかうらわ

Bessho
別所

Kishi-machi
岸町

Minami-Urawa
南浦和

Urawa Tech.H.Sch.
浦和工高

Seki
関

Shinmei
神明

To Shin-mat
至しん

Sakurada
桜田

Shikatebukuro
鹿手袋

Minami-Ur
みなみうら

7

MUSASHINO LINE 武蔵野線

Nishi-Urawa
にしうらわ

Musashi-Urawa
むさしうらわ

NTT

To Fuchū-honmachi
至ふちゅうほんまち

To Ikebukuro 至いけぶくろ

To Ueno
至うえの

A   B   C   D

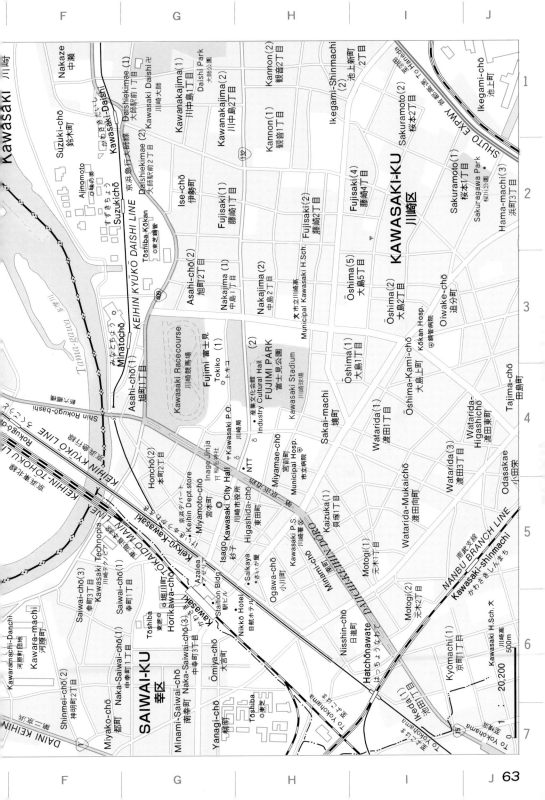

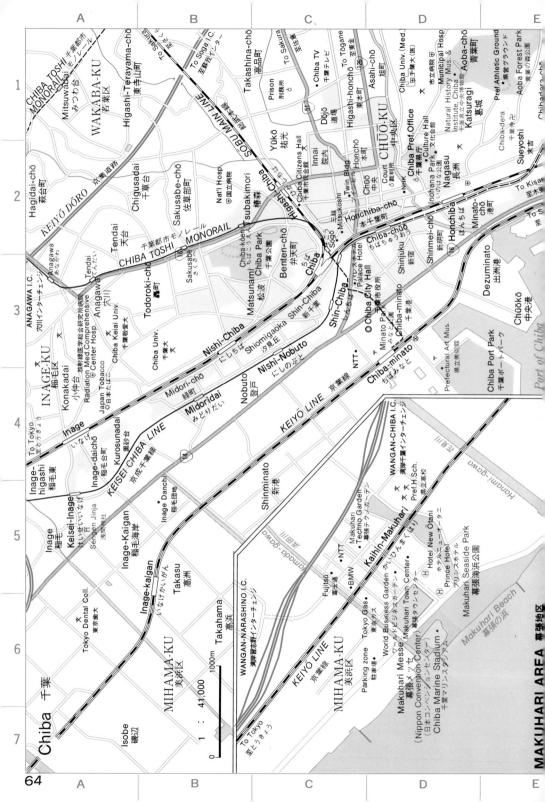

INDEX
索　引（ABC順）

Government Offices
官公庁

Agency for Cultural Affairs　文化庁	03-3581-4211	
Agency of Natural Resources & Energy	03-3501-1511	
資源エネルギー庁		
Board of Audit　会計検査院	03-3581-3251	
Defense Agency　防衛庁	03-3408-5211	
Defense Facilities Administration Agency	03-3408-5211	
防衛施設庁		
Economic Planning Agency　経済企画庁	03-3581-0261	
Environment Agency　環境庁	03-3581-3351	
Fair Trade Commission　公正取引委員会	03-3581-5471	
Fire Defense Agency　消防庁	03-3581-5311	
Fisheries Agency　水産庁	03-3502-8111	
Food Agency　食糧庁	03-3502-8111	
Forestry Agency　林野庁	03-3502-8111	
Hokkaidō Development Agency	03-3581-9111	
北海道開発庁		
House of Councillors　参議院	03-3581-3111	
House of Representatives　衆議院	03-3581-5111	
Imperial Household Agency　宮内庁	03-3213-1111	
Japan Academy　日本学士院	03-3822-2101	
Japan Art Academy　日本芸術院	03-3821-7191	
Management & Coordination Agency	03-3581-6361	
総務庁		
Maritime Safety Agency　海上保安庁	03-3591-6361	
Meteorological Agency　気象庁	03-3212-8341	
Metropolitan Police Dept.　警視庁	03-3581-4321	
Ministry of Agriculture Forestry & Fisheries		
農林水産省	03-3502-8111	
Ministry of Construction　建設省	03-3580-4311	
Ministry of Education　文部省	03-3581-4211	
Ministry of Finance　大蔵省	03-3581-4111	
Ministry of Foreign Affairs　外務省	03-3580-3311	
Ministry of Health & Welfare　厚生省	03-3503-1711	
Ministry of Home Affairs　自治省	03-3581-5311	
Ministry of Int'l Trade & Industry	03-3501-1511	
通商産業省		
Ministry of Justice　法務省	03-3580-4111	
Ministry of Labor　労働省	03-3593-1211	
Ministry of Posts & Telecommunications	03-3504-4411	
郵政省		

Ministry of Transport　運輸省	03-3580-3111
National Diet Library　国立国会図書館	03-3581-2331
National Institute of Health	03-3444-2181
国立予防衛生研究所	
National Land Agency　国土庁	03-3593-3311
National Personnel Authority　人事院	03-3581-5311
National Police Agency　警察庁	03-3581-0141
National Public Safety Commission	03-3581-0141
国家公安委員会	
National Tax Administration Agency	03-3581-4161
国税庁	
Okinawa Development Agency	03-3581-2361
沖縄開発庁	
Patent Office　特許庁	03-3581-1101
Prime Minister's Office　総理府	03-3581-2361
Prime Minister's Official Residence	03-3581-0101
内閣総理大臣官邸	
Printing Bureau　大蔵省印刷局	03-3582-4411
Public Prosecutor's Office　検察庁	03-3592-5611
Science Council of Japan　日本学術会議	03-3403-6291
Science & Technology Agency　科学技術庁	03-3581-5271
Small & Medium Enterprise Agency	03-3501-1511
中小企業庁	
Social Insurance Agency　社会保険庁	03-3503-1711
Supreme Court　最高裁判所	03-3264-8111
Tokyo Customshouse　東京税関	03-3472-7000
Tokyo District Court　東京地方裁判所	03-3581-5411
Tokyo High Court　東京高等裁判所	03-3581-5411
Tokyo Metropolitan Government　東京都庁	03-5321-1111
Tokyo Regional Immigration Bureau	03-3213-8111
東京入国管理局	
Yokohama Customshouse　横浜税関	045-201-4981

Tokyo 23 Wards　東京23区
〔Ward Offices　区役所〕

Adachi　足立	03-3882-1111
Arakawa　荒川	03-3802-3111
Bunkyō　文京	03-3812-7111
Chiyoda　千代田	03-3264-0151
Cyūō　中央	03-3543-0211

Edogawa 江戸川	03-3652-1151	Hinode 日の出	0425-97-0511
Itabashi 板橋	03-3964-1111	Itsukaichi 五日市	0425-96-1511
Katsushika · 葛飾	03-3695-1111	Mizuho 瑞穂	0425-57-0501
Kita 北	03-3908-1111	Okutama 奥多摩	0428-83-2111
Kōtō 江東	03-3647-9111		
Meguro 目黒	03-3715-1111	**Kanagawa Pref.** 神奈川県	
Minato 港	03-3578-2111	〔City Offices 市役所〕	
Nakano 中野	03-3389-1111	Atsugi 厚木	0462-23-1511
Nerima 練馬	03-3993-1111	Ayase 綾瀬	0467-77-1111
Ōta 大田	03-3773-5111	Chigasaki 茅ヶ崎	0467-82-1111
Setagaya 世田谷	03-3412-1111	Ebina 海老名	0462-31-2111
Shibuya 渋谷	03-3463-1211	Fujisawa 藤沢	0466-25-1111
Shinagawa 品川	03-3777-1111	Hadano 秦野	0463-82-5111
Shinjuku 新宿	03-3209-1111	Hiratsuka 平塚	0463-23-1111
Suginami 杉並	03-3312-2111	Isehara 伊勢原	0463-94-4711
Sumida 墨田	03-5608-1111	Kamakura 鎌倉	0467-23-3000
Taitō 台東	03-5246-1111	Kawasaki 川崎	044-200-2111
Toshima 豊島	03-3981-1111	Minami-ashigara 南足柄	0465-74-2111
		Miura 三浦	0468-82-1111
Tokyo Tama Area 東京多摩地区		Odawara 小田原	0465-33-1381
〔City Offices 市役所〕		Sagamihara 相模原	0427-54-1111
Akigawa 秋川	0425-58-1111	Yamato 大和	0462-63-1111
Akishima 昭島	0425-44-5111	Yokohama 横浜	045-671-2121
Chōfu 調布	0424-81-7111	Yokosuka 横須賀	0468-22-4000
Fuchū 府中	0423-64-4111	Zama 座間	0462-55-1111
Fussa 福生	0425-51-1511	Zushi 逗子	0468-73-1111
Hachiōji 八王子	0426-26-3111		
Hamura 羽村	0425-55-1111	〔Town Offices 町役場〕	
Higashi-kurume 東久留米	0424-73-5111	Aikawa 愛川	0462-85-2111
Higashi-murayama 東村山	0423-93-5111	Fujino 藤野	0426-87-2111
Higashi-yamato 東大和	0425-63-2111	Hakone 箱根	0460-5-7111
Hino 日野	0425-85-1111	Hayama 葉山	0468-76-1111
Hōya 保谷	0424-21-2525	Kaisei 開成	0465-83-2331
Inagi 稲城	0423-78-2111	Manazuru 真鶴	0465-68-1131
Kiyose 清瀬	0424-92-5111	Matsuda 松田	0465-83-1221
Kodaira 小平	0423-41-1211	Nakai 中井	0465-81-1111
Koganei 小金井	0423-83-1111	Ninomiya 二宮	0463-71-3311
Kokubunji 国分寺	0423-25-0111	Ōi 大井	0465-83-1311
Komae 狛江	03-3430-1111	Ōiso 大磯	0463-61-4100
Kunitachi 国立	0425-76-2111	Sagamiko 相模湖	0426-84-3211
Machida 町田	0427-22-3111	Samukawa 寒川	0467-74-1111
Mitaka 三鷹	0422-45-1151	Shiroyama 城山	0427-82-1111
Musashi-murayama 武蔵村山	0425-65-1111	Tsukui 津久井	0427-84-1141
Musashino 武蔵野	0422-51-5131	Yamakita 山北	0465-75-1122
Ōme 青梅	0428-22-1111	Yugawara 湯河原	0465-63-2111
Tachikawa 立川	0425-23-2111		
Tama 多摩	0423-75-8111	**Saitama Pref.** 埼玉県	
Tanashi 田無	0424-64-1311	〔City Offices 市役所〕	
		Ageo 上尾	048-775-5111
〔Town Offices 町役場〕		Asaka 朝霞	048-463-1111

Chichibu　秩父	0494-22-2211
Fujimi　富士見	0492-51-2711
Fukaya　深谷	0485-71-1211
Gyōda　行田	0485-56-1111
Hannō　飯能	0429-73-2111
Hanyū　羽生	0485-61-1121
Hasuda　蓮田	048-768-3111
Hatogaya　鳩ヶ谷	048-285-1111
Hidaka　日高	0429-89-2111
Higashi-matsuyama　東松山	0493-23-2221
Honjō　本庄	0495-24-5151
Iruma　入間	0429-64-1111
Iwatsuki　岩槻	048-757-4111
Kamifukuoka　上福岡	0492-61-2611
Kasukabe　春日部	048-736-1111
Kawagoe　川越	0492-24-8811
Kawaguchi　川口	048-252-0251
Kazo　加須	0480-62-1111
Kitamoto　北本	0485-91-1711
Kōnosu　鴻巣	0485-41-1321
Koshigaya　越谷	0489-64-2111
Kuki　久喜	0480-22-1111
Kumagaya　熊谷	0485-24-1111
Misato　三郷	0489-53-1111
Niiza　新座	048-477-1111
Okegawa　桶川	048-786-3211
Ōmiya　大宮	048-643-4321
Sakado　坂戸	0492-83-1331
Satte　幸手	0480-43-1111
Sayama　狭山	0429-53-1111
Shiki　志木	048-473-1111
Sōka　草加	0489-22-0151
Toda　戸田	048-441-1800
Tokorozawa　所沢	0429-98-1111
Tsurugashima　鶴ヶ島	0492-71-1111
Urawa　浦和	048-833-0411
Wakō　和光	048-464-1111
Warabi　蕨	048-432-3200
Yashio　八潮	0489-96-2111
Yono　与野	048-853-2211

Ibaraki Pref.　茨城県
〔City Offices　市役所〕

Hitachi　日立	0294-22-3111
Hitachiōta　常陸太田	0294-72-3111
Ishioka　石岡	02992-3-1111
Iwai　岩井	0297-35-2121
Kasama　笠間	0296-72-1111
Katsuta　勝田	0292-73-0111
Kita-ibaraki　北茨城	0293-43-1111

Koga　古河	0280-22-5111
Mito　水戸	0292-24-1111
Mitsukaidō　水海道	02972-3-2111
Nakaminato　那珂湊	0292-62-4121
Ryūgasaki　龍ヶ崎	0297-64-1111
Shimodate　下館	0296-24-2111
Shimotsuma　下妻	0296-43-2111
Takahagi　高萩	0293-23-2111
Toride　取手	0297-74-2141
Tsuchiura　土浦	0298-21-3510
Tsukuba　つくば	0298-36-1111
Ushiku　牛久	0298-73-2111
Yūki　結城	0296-32-1111

Tochigi Pref.　栃木県
〔City Offices　市役所〕

Ashikaga　足利	0284-21-1141
Imaichi　今市	0288-22-1111
Kanuma　鹿沼	0289-64-2111
Kuroiso　黒磯	0287-63-1111
Mōka　真岡	0285-82-1111
Nikkō　日光	0288-54-1111
Ōtawara　大田原	0287-23-1111
Oyama　小山	0285-23-1111
Sano　佐野	0283-24-5111
Tochigi　栃木	0282-22-3535
Utsunomiya　宇都宮	0286-32-2222
Yaita　矢板	0287-43-1111

Gunma Pref.　群馬県
〔City Offices　市役所〕

Annaka　安中	0273-82-1111
Fujioka　藤岡	0274-22-1211
Isesaki　伊勢崎	0270-24-5111
Kiryū　桐生	0277-46-1111
Maebashi　前橋	0272-24-1111
Numata　沼田	0278-23-2111
Ōta　太田	0276-45-8181
Shibukawa　渋川	0279-22-2111
Takasaki　高崎	0273-23-5511
Tatebayashi　館林	0276-72-4111
Tomioka　富岡	0274-62-1511

Yamanashi Pref.　山梨県
〔City Offices　市役所〕

Enzan　塩山	0553-32-2111
Fujiyoshida　富士吉田	0555-22-1111
Kōfu　甲府	0552-37-1161
Ōtsuki　大月	0554-22-2111
Tsuru　都留	0554-43-1111
Yamanashi　山梨	0553-22-1111

Hotels and Inns
ホテル，旅館

〔Tokyo　東京〕

Akasaka Prince H.　赤坂プリンスホテル	03-3234-1111
Akasaka Shanpia H.	03-3586-0811
赤坂シャンピアホテル	
Akasaka Tōkyū H.　赤坂東急ホテル	03-3580-2311
Akasaka Yōkō H.　赤坂陽光ホテル	03-3586-4050
Akihabara Washington H.	03-3255-3311
秋葉原ワシントンホテル	
ANA H. Tokyo　東京全日空ホテル	03-3505-1111
Aoi Grand H.　葵グランドホテル	03-3946-2721
Aoyama Shanpia H.　青山シャンピアホテル	03-3407-2111
Asakusa View H.　浅草ビューホテル	03-3842-2111
Asia Center of Japan　アジア会館	03-3402-6111
Atagoyama Tōkyū Inn　愛宕山東急イン	03-3431-0109
Azabu City H.　麻布シティホテル	03-3453-4311
Business H. Nihombashi Villa	03-3668-0840
ビジネスホテル日本橋ヴィラ	
Capitol Tōkyū H.　キャピトル東急ホテル	03-3581-4511
Center H. Tokyo　センターホテル東京	03-3667-2711
Central H.　セントラルホテル	03-3256-6251
Co-op Inn Shibuya　コープ・イン渋谷	03-3486-6600
Diamond H.　ダイヤモンドホテル	03-3263-2211
Fairmont H.　フェヤーモントホテル	03-3262-1151
Gajoen Kankō H.　雅叙園観光ホテル	03-3491-0111
Ginza Capital H.　銀座キャピタルホテル	03-3543-8211
Ginza Daiichi H.　銀座第一ホテル	03-3542-5311
Ginza Int'l H.　銀座国際ホテル	03-3574-1121
Ginza Marunouchi H.　銀座丸ノ内ホテル	03-3543-5431
Ginza Nikkō H.　銀座日航ホテル	03-3571-4911
Ginza Tōbu H.　銀座東武ホテル	03-3546-0111
Ginza Tōkyū H.　銀座東急ホテル	03-3541-2411
Goten-yama Hills H. Laforet Tokyo	03-5488-3911
御殿山ヒルズホテルラフォーレ東京	
Grand Central H.	03-3256-3211
グランドセントラルホテル	
Haneda Tōkyū H.　羽田東急ホテル	03-3747-0311
Harumi Grand H.　晴海グランドホテル	03-3533-7111
Hill Port H.　ヒルポートホテル	03-3462-5171
Hilltop (Yamanoue) H.　山の上ホテル	03-3293-2311
Holiday Inn Tokyo　ホリデイ・イン東京	03-3553-6161

H. Century Hyatt	03-3349-0111
ホテルセンチュリーハイアット	
H. Dai-ei　ホテルダイエー	03-3813-6271
H. Edmont　ホテルエドモント	03-3237-1111
H. Friend　ホテルフレンド	03-3866-2244
H. Ginza Dai-ei　ホテル銀座ダイエー	03-3545-1111
H. Grand Business	03-3984-5121
ホテルグランドビジネス	
H. Grand Palace　ホテルグランドパレス	03-3264-1111
H. Ibis　ホテルアイビス	03-3403-4411
H. Kayū Kaikan　ホテル霞友会館	03-3230-1111
H. Kizankan　ホテル機山館	03-3812-1211
H. Kokusai Kankō　ホテル国際観光	03-3215-3281
H. Lungwood　ホテルラングウッド	03-3803-1234
H. Metropolitan　ホテルメトロポリタン	03-3980-1111
H. Mita Kaikan　ホテル三田会館	03-3453-6601
H. New Grand Hachiōji	0426-45-0015
ホテルニューグランド八王子	
H. New Meguro　ホテルニューメグロ	03-3719-8121
H. New Ōtani　ホテルニューオータニ	03-3265-1111
H. New Tokyo　ホテルニュー東京	03-3469-5211
H. Ōkura　ホテルオークラ	03-3582-0111
H. Pacific Meridien Tokyo	03-3445-6711
ホテルパシフィック東京	
H. Park Lane Nishikasai	03-3675-8900
ホテルパークレーン西葛西	
H. President Aoyama	03-3497-0111
ホテルプレジデント青山	
H. Satoh　ホテルサトー	03-3815-1133
H. Seaside Edogawa	03-3804-1180
ホテルシーサイド江戸川	
H. Seiyō Ginza　ホテル西洋銀座	03-3585-1111
H. Sun City Ikebukuro	03-3986-1101
ホテルサンシティ池袋	
H. Sunlite Shinjuku　ホテルサンライト新宿	03-3356-0391
H. Sunroute Ikebukuro	03-3980-1911
ホテルサンルート池袋	
H. Sunroute Shibuya	03-3464-6411
ホテルサンルート渋谷	
H. Sunroute Tokyo　ホテルサンルート東京	03-3375-3211

H. Takanawa　ホテル高輪	03-5488-1000	
H. Tokyo　ホテル東京	03-3447-5771	
H. Tōkyū Kankō　ホテル東急観光	03-3582-0451	
H. Tōyō　ホテル東陽	03-3615-1041	
H. Universal Nihombashi-Kayabachō	03-3668-7711	
ホテルユニバーサル日本橋茅場町		
H. Yaesu Ryūmeikan　ホテル八重洲竜名館	03-3271-0971	
Ikebukuro Centercity H.	03-3985-1311	
池袋センターシティホテル		
Ikebukuro H. Theatre　池袋ホテルテアトル	03-3988-2251	
Ikenohata Bunka Center	03-3822-0151	
池之端文化センター		
Imperial Hotel (Teikoku Hotel)　帝国ホテル	03-3504-1111	
Kadoya H.　かどやホテル	03-3346-2561	
Kayabachō Pearl H.　茅場町パールホテル	03-3553-2211	
Keiō Plaza H.　京王プラザホテル	03-3344-0111	
Kichijōji Tōkyū Inn　吉祥寺東急イン	0422-47-0109	
Marroad Inn Akasaka　マロウド・イン赤坂	03-3585-7611	
Mitsui Urban H. Ginza	03-3572-4131	
三井アーバンホテル銀座		
Miyako H. Tokyo　都ホテル東京	03-3447-3111	
Miyako Inn Tokyo　都イン東京	03-3454-3111	
New Central H.　ニューセントラルホテル	03-3256-2171	
New Ōtani Inn Tokyo	03-3779-9111	
ニューオータニイン東京		
New Takanawa Prince H.	03-3442-1111	
新高輪プリンスホテル		
Nihon Seinenkan H.　日本青年館ホテル	03-3401-0101	
Ochanomizu Inn　お茶の水イン	03-3813-8211	
Ōmori Tōkyū Inn　大森東急イン	03-3768-0109	
Palace H.　パレスホテル	03-3211-5211	
Roppongi Prince H.　六本木プリンスホテル	03-3587-1111	
Royal Park H.　ロイヤルパークホテル	03-3667-1111	
Ryōgoku Pearl H.　両国パールホテル	03-3626-3211	
Ryōgoku River H.　両国リバーホテル	03-3634-1711	
Satellite H. Kōrakuen	03-3814-0202	
サテライトホテル後楽園		
Shiba Park H.　芝パークホテル	03-3433-4141	
Shibuya Business H.　渋谷ビジネスホテル	03-3409-9300	
Shibuya Tōbu H.　渋谷東武ホテル	03-3476-0111	
Shibuya Tōkyū Inn　渋谷東急イン	03-3498-0109	
Shinagawa Prince H.　品川プリンスホテル	03-3440-1111	
Shinjuku New City H.	03-3375-6511	
新宿ニューシティホテル		
Shinjuku Park H.　新宿パークホテル	03-3356-0241	
Shinjuku Prince H.　新宿プリンスホテル	03-3205-1111	
Shinjuku Sun Park H.	03-3362-7101	
新宿サンパークホテル		
Shinjuku Washington H.	03-3343-3111	
新宿ワシントンホテル		

Star H. Tokyo　スターホテル東京	03-3361-1111	
Suidōbashi Grand H.	03-3816-2101	
水道橋グランドホテル		
Suigetsu H.　水月ホテル	03-3822-4611	
Sunshine City Prince H.	03-3988-1111	
サンシャインシティプリンスホテル		
Taishō Central H.　大正セントラルホテル	03-3232-0101	
Takanawa Prince H.　高輪プリンスホテル	03-3447-1111	
Takanawa Tōbu H.　高輪東武ホテル	03-3447-0111	
Teikoku H. (Imperial H.)　帝国ホテル	03-3504-1111	
Tōkō H.　東興ホテル	03-3494-1050	
Tokyo Business H.　東京ビジネスホテル	03-3356-4605	
Tokyo City H.　東京シティーホテル	03-3270-7671	
Tokyo Grand H.　東京グランドホテル	03-3454-0311	
Tokyo Green H. Awajichō	03-3255-4161	
東京グリーンホテル淡路町		
Tokyo Green H. Kōrakuen	03-3816-4161	
東京グリーンホテル後楽園		
Tokyo Green H. Suidōbashi	03-3295-4161	
東京グリーンホテル水道橋		
Tokyo Hilton International	03-3344-5111	
東京ヒルトンインターナショナル		
Tokyo H. Urashima　東京ホテル浦島	03-3533-3111	
Tokyo Koma Ryokō Kaikan	03-3585-1046	
東京コマ旅行会館		
Tokyo Marunouchi H.　東京丸ノ内ホテル	03-3215-2151	
Tokyo Prince H.　東京プリンスホテル	03-3432-1111	
Tokyo Station H.　東京ステーションホテル	03-3231-2511	
Tokyo Sunny Side H.	03-3649-1211	
東京サニーサイドホテル		
Tokyo YMCA H.　東京YMCAホテル	03-3293-1911	
Toshi Center H.　都市センターホテル	03-3265-8211	
Tsukuba H.　ツクバホテル	03-3834-2556	
Ueno Terminal H.　上野ターミナルホテル	03-3831-1110	
Yaesu Fujiya H.　八重洲富士屋ホテル	03-3273-2111	
Yomiuri Land Kaikan　よみうりランド会館	044-966-1137	

〔Yokohama　横浜〕

Aster H.　アスターホテル	045-651-0141	
Bund H.　バンドホテル	045-621-1101	
Central Inn Yokohama	045-251-1010	
セントラルイン横浜		
Fuji View H. Shin-Yokohama	045-473-0021	
フジビューホテル新横浜		
Holiday Inn Yokohama　ホリデイ・イン横浜	045-681-3311	
H. Cosmo Yokohama　ホテルコスモ横浜	045-314-3111	
H. Empire　ホテルエンパイア	045-851-1431	
H. New Grand　ホテルニューグランド	045-681-1841	
H. Park Lane Tsurumi	045-504-8900	
ホテルパークレーン鶴見		

H. Rich Yokohama　ホテルリッチ横浜	045-312-2111	
H. Yokohama Garden　ホテル横浜ガーデン	045-641-1311	
International Plaza H.	045-664-1133	
インターナショナルプラザホテル		
New Ōtani Inn Yokohama	045-252-1311	
ニューオータニイン横浜		
Satellite H. Yokohama	045-641-0202	
サテライトホテル横浜		
Shin-Yokohama H.　新横浜ホテル	045-471-6011	
Shin-Yokohama Kokusai H.	045-473-1311	
新横浜国際ホテル		
Shin-Yokohama Prince H.	045-471-1111	
新横浜プリンスホテル		
Star H. Yokohama　スターホテル横浜	045-651-3111	
The H. Yokohama　ザ・ホテルヨコハマ	045-662-1321	
Tsurumi Pearl H.　鶴見パールホテル	045-501-8080	
Yokohama Grand Intercontinental H.	045-223-2222	
ヨコハマグランドインターコンチネンタルホテル		
Yokohama-Isezakichō Washington H.	045-243-7111	
横浜伊勢佐木町ワシントンホテル		
Yokohama Kokusai H.　横浜国際ホテル	045-311-1311	
Yokohama Prince H.　横浜プリンスホテル	045-751-1111	
Yokohama Tōkyū H.　横浜東急ホテル	045-311-1682	

〔Kawasaki　川崎〕

Heiwa Plaza H.　平和プラザホテル	044-222-3131
H. Sun Royal Kawasaki	044-244-3711
ホテルサンロイヤル川崎	
Kawasaki Grand H.　川崎グランドホテル	044-244-2111
Kawasaki H. Park　川崎ホテルパーク	044-211-5885
Kawasaki Nikkō H.　川崎日航ホテル	044-244-5941
Tōyoko Inn Kawasaki-ekimaehonchō	044-246-1045
東横イン川崎駅前本町	

〔Yokosuka　横須賀〕

H. Centraza Yokosuka	0468-27-1111
ホテルセントラーザ横須賀	
H. New Yokosuka　ホテルニューヨコスカ	0468-25-2211
H. Yokosuka　ホテル横須賀	0468-25-1111

〔Shōnan　湘南〕

Hokke Club Fujisawa　法華クラブ藤沢店	0466-27-6101
H. Sunroute Hiratsuka	0463-21-7111
ホテルサンルート平塚	
Kamakura Park H.　鎌倉パークホテル	0467-25-5121
Ōiso Prince H.　大磯プリンスホテル	0463-61-7111

〔Chiba　千葉〕

Birdie H. Chiba　バーディーホテル千葉	043-248-5551
Chiba Grand H.　千葉グランドホテル	043-241-2111

Chiba Keisei H.　千葉京成ホテル	043-222-2111
Chiba New Park H.	043-242-1111
千葉ニューパークホテル	
Chiba Palace H.　千葉パレスホテル	043-247-1111
Chiba Pearl H.　千葉パールホテル	043-247-8080
Chiba Star H.　千葉スターホテル	043-246-2332
Chiba Washington H.	043-222-4511
千葉ワシントンホテル	
H. New Tsukamoto　ホテルニューツカモト	043-243-1111
H. Sun City Chiba　ホテルサンシティ千葉	043-247-1101
H. Sun Garden Chiba	043-224-1131
ホテルサンガーデン千葉	
Plaza H.　プラザホテル	043-241-8051
Royal Plaza H.　ロイヤルプラザホテル	043-224-6111

〔Makuhari Area　幕張地区〕

H. Francs　ホテルフランクス	047-296-2111
H. Green Tower Makuhari	047-296-1122
ホテルグリーンタワー幕張	
H. New Ōtani Makuhari	043-297-7777
ホテルニューオータニ幕張（Open fall '93)	
H. Springs Makuhari	047-296-3111
ホテルスプリングス幕張	
H. The Manhattan　ホテル・ザ・マンハッタン	047-275-1111
Makuhari Prince H.　幕張プリンスホテル	047-296-1111
Tōyoko Inn Chiba Makuhari	047-242-1045
東横イン千葉幕張	

〔Naita　成田〕

ANA H. Narita　成田全日空ホテル	0476-33-1311
Holiday Inn Tōbu Narita	0476-32-1234
ホリデイイン東武成田	
H. Centraza Narita	0476-93-8811
ホテルセントラーザ成田	
H. Nikkō Narita　ホテル日航成田	0476-32-0032
Narita Airport Resthouse	0476-32-1212
成田エアポートレストハウス	
Narita International H.	0476-93-1234
成田インターナショナルホテル	
Narita Tōkyū Inn　成田東急イン	0476-33-0109
Narita View H.　成田ビューホテル	0476-32-1111
Narita Wins H.　成田ウィンズホテル	0476-33-1111

〔Urayasu　浦安〕

Dai-ichi H. Tokyo Bay　第一ホテル東京ベイ	0473-55-3333
Sheraton Grande Tokyo Bay H.	0473-55-5555
シェラトングランデトーキョーベイホテル	
Sunroute Plaza Tokyo	0473-55-1111
サンルートプラザ東京	
Tokyo Bay Hilton　東京ベイヒルトン	0473-55-5000

Tokyo Bay H. Tōkyū　東京ベイホテル東急	0473-55-2411	Utsunomiya Central H.	0286-25-1717
		宇都宮セントラルホテル	
〔Mito　水戸〕		Utsunomiya Grand H.	0286-35-2111
Mito Keisei H.　水戸京成ホテル	0292-26-3111	宇都宮グランドホテル	
Mito Plaza H.　水戸プラザホテル	0292-31-8111	Utsunomiya Royal H.	0286-33-0331
Mito Prince H.　水戸プリンスホテル	0292-27-4111	宇都宮ロイヤルホテル	
Sannomaru H.　三の丸ホテル	0292-21-3011	Utsunomiya Tōbu H.　宇都宮東武ホテル	0286-36-3063
		Utsunomiya Washington H.	0286-21-3111
〔Tsukuba　つくば〕		宇都宮ワシントンホテル	
H. Sunroute Tsukuba	0298-52-1151		
ホテルサンルートつくば		〔Maebashi　前橋〕	
H. Suwa　ホテルスワ	0298-36-4011	Gunma Royal H.　群馬ロイヤルホテル	0272-23-6111
Tsukuba Dai-ichi H.　筑波第一ホテル	0298-52-1112	Maebashi Tōkyū Inn　前橋東急イン	0272-21-0109
Tsukuba Sky H.　つくばスカイホテル	0298-51-0008	Maebashi Yūai H.　前橋ユーアイホテル	0272-23-0211
		Mercury H.　マーキュリーホテル	0272-52-0111
〔Utsunomiya　宇都宮〕			
H. Maruji　ホテル丸治	0286-21-2211	〔Saitama　埼玉〕	
H. New Itaya　ホテルニューイタヤ	0286-35-5511	Kawagoe Tōbu H.　川越東武ホテル	0492-25-0111
H. Sunroute Utsunomiya	0286-21-3355	Marroad Inn Ōmiya　マロウドイン大宮	048-645-5111
ホテルサンルート宇都宮		Ōmiya Pioland H.　大宮パイオランドホテル	048-648-0010
H. Sun Royal Utsunomiya	0286-38-3711	Palace H. Ōmiya　パレスホテル大宮	048-647-3300
ホテルサン・ロイヤル宇都宮		Plaza H. Urawa　プラザホテル浦和	048-863-5111
Kantō Chisan H. Utsunomiya	0286-34-4311	Urawa Tōbu H.　浦和東武ホテル	048-825-4711
関東チサンホテル宇都宮			

Japanese Inn Group
ジャパニーズ・イン・グループ

〔Tokyo　東京〕		Petit H. Ebisuya　プチホテルエビスヤ	0555-72-0165
(Asakusa) Kikuya Ryokan　喜久屋旅館	03-3841-6404		
浅草		〔Hakone　箱根〕	
(Koiwa) Ryokan Kaneda　旅館金田	03-3657-1747	Fuji-Hakone Guest House	0460-4-6577
小岩		富士箱根ゲストハウス	
(Ueno) Ryokan Katsutarō　旅館勝太郎	03-3821-9808	Moto-Hakone Guest House	0460-3-7880
上野		元箱根ゲストハウス	
Ryokan Mikawaya Bekkan　旅館三河屋別館	03-3843-2345		
(Gotanda) Ryokan Sansuisō　旅館山水荘	03-3441-7475	〔Zushi　逗子〕	
五反田		Shindō-tei Ryokan　新道亭旅館	0468-71-2012
Sakura Ryokan　桜旅館	03-3876-8118		
Sawanoya Ryokan　澤の屋旅館	03-3822-2251	〔Nikkō　日光〕	
(Okutama) Shukubō: Komadori-Sansō	0428-78-8472	Lodging-house St.Bois	0288-53-0082
奥多摩　　　　駒鳥山荘		ロッジングハウスサンボワ	
Suigetsu H./Ōgaisō　水月ホテル/鴎外荘	03-3822-4611	Pension Turtle　ペンション・タートル	0288-53-3168
〔Lake Kawaguchi　河口湖〕		〔Mito　水戸〕	
H. Ashiwada　足和田ホテル	0555-82-2321	Ryokan-Izumi-sō　旅館いづみ荘	0292-21-3504

Youth Hostels
ユースホステル

〔Tokyo 東京〕
Hachiōji Youth Guesthouse	0426-48-2111
八王子ユースゲストハウス	
Mitake 御岳	0428-78-8501
Takao 高尾	0426-61-0437
Tokyo Kokusai 東京国際	03-3235-1107
Tokyo Yoyogi 東京代々木	03-3467-9163

〔Kanagawa 神奈川〕
Hakone Sōunzan 箱根早雲山	0460-2-3827
Jōgashima 城ヶ島	0468-81-3893
Kamakura Kagetsuen 鎌倉花月園	0467-25-1238
Kanagawa 神奈川	045-241-6503
Manazuru 真鶴	0465-68-3580
Sagamiko 相模湖	0426-84-2338
Shōnan 湘南	0467-82-2401

〔Saitama 埼玉〕
Chichibu 秩父	0494-55-0056
Kamakita-ko 鎌北湖	0492-94-0219

〔Chiba 千葉〕
Chiba-shi 千葉市	0472-94-1850
Kujūkurihama Shirako 九十九里浜白子	0475-33-2254
Tateyama 館山	0470-28-0073

〔Ibaraki 茨城〕
Kaba-sansō 加波山荘	0296-55-1928
Mito Tokuda 水戸徳田	0296-7-3113

〔Tsuchiura Masuo 土浦増尾〕 0298-21-4430
Tsukuba-san 筑波山	0296-54-1200
Tsukuba-sansō 筑波山荘	0298-66-0022

〔Tochigi 栃木〕
Nasu-Kōgen 那須高原	0287-76-1615
Nikkō 日光	0288-54-1013
Nikkō Daiyagawa 日光大谷川	0288-54-1974
Shinkōen 真光苑	0288-26-0951

〔Gunma 群馬〕
Akagi-paos 赤城パオス	0279-56-5731
Haruna-kōgen 榛名高原	0273-74-9300
Kusatsu-kōgen 草津高原	0279-88-3895
Oze Tokura 尾瀬戸倉	0278-58-7421

〔Yamanashi 山梨〕
Dōshikan 道志館	0554-52-2015
Fuji-Saiko 富士西湖	0555-82-2616
Fujiyoshida 富士吉田	0555-22-0533
Isawa-onsen 石和温泉	0552-62-2110
Kawaguchi-ko 河口湖	0555-72-1431
Kōfu 甲府	0552-51-8020
Yamanakako Marimo 山中湖マリモ	0555-62-4210

〔Shizuoka 静岡〕
Gotenba 御殿場	0550-82-3045
Itō 伊東	0557-45-0224
Shuzenji 修善寺	0558-72-1222

Embassies
大使館

Algeria アルジェリア	03-3711-2661	
Argentina アルゼンチン	03-5420-7101	
Australia オーストラリア	03-5232-4111	
Austria オーストリア	03-3451-8281	
Bangladesh バングラデシュ	03-3442-1501	
Belgium ベルギー	03-3262-0191	
Bolivia ボリビア	03-3499-5441	
Brazil ブラジル	03-3404-5211	
Britain (United Kingdom) イギリス	03-3265-5511	
Brunei ブルネイ	03-3447-7997	
Bulgaria ブルガリア	03-3465-1021	
Burundi ブルンジ	03-3443-7321	
Cameroon カメルーン	03-3496-4101	
Canada カナダ	03-3408-2101	
Central African Rep. 中央アフリカ	03-3485-7591	
Chili チリ	03-3452-7561	
China 中華人民共和国	03-3403-3380	
Colombia コロンビア	03-3440-6451	
Costa Rica コスタリカ	03-3486-1812	
Côte d'Ivoire コートジボアール	03-3499-7021	
Cuba キューバ	03-3716-3112	
Czecho チェコ	03-3400-8122	
Denmark デンマーク	03-3496-3001	
Djibouti ジブチ	03-3496-6135	
Dominican Rep. ドミニカ共和国	03-3499-6020	
EC-Delegation 駐日EC委員会	03-3239-0441	
Ecuador エクアドル	03-3499-2800	
Egypt エジプト	03-3770-8022	
El Salvador エルサルバドル	03-3499-4461	
Ethiopia エチオピア	03-3718-1003	
Fiji フィジー	03-3587-2038	
Finland フィンランド	03-3442-2231	
France フランス	03-3473-0171	
Gabon ガボン	03-3448-9540	
Germany ドイツ	03-3473-0151	
Ghana ガーナ	03-3710-8831	
Greece ギリシア	03-3403-0871	
Guatemala グアテマラ	03-3400-1830	
Guinea ギニア	03-3769-0451	
Haiti ハイチ	03-3486-7070	
Honduras ホンジュラス	03-3401-1150	
Hungary ハンガリー	03-3798-8801	
India インド	03-3262-2391	
Indonesia インドネシア	03-3441-4201	
Iran イラン	03-3446-8011	
Iraq イラク	03-3423-1727	
Ireland アイルランド	03-3263-0695	
Israel イスラエル	03-3264-0911	
Italy イタリア	03-3453-5291	
Jordan ヨルダン	03-3580-5856	
Kenya ケニア	03-3723-4006	
Korea (South) 大韓民国	03-3452-7611	
Kuwait クウェート	03-3455-0361	
Laos ラオス	03-5411-2291	
Lebanon レバノン	03-3580-1227	
Liberia リベリア	03-3441-7138	
Libya リビア	03-3477-0701	
Luxembourg ルクセンブルク	03-3265-9621	
Madagascar マダガスカル	03-3446-7252	
Malaysia マレーシア	03-3476-3840	
Mauritania モーリタニア	03-3449-3822	
Mexico メキシコ	03-3581-1131	
Micronesia ミクロネシア連邦	03-3585-5456	
Mongolia モンゴル	03-3469-2088	
Morocco モロッコ	03-3478-3271	
Myanmar ミャンマー	03-3441-9291	
Nepal ネパール	03-3705-5558	
Netherlands オランダ	03-5401-0411	
New Zealand ニュージーランド	03-3467-2271	
Nicaragua ニカラグア	03-3499-0400	
Nigeria ナイジェリア	03-3468-5531	
Norway ノルウェー	03-3440-2611	
Oman オマーン	03-3402-0877	
Pakistan パキスタン	03-3454-4861	
Panama パナマ	03-3499-3741	
Papua New Guinea パプア・ニューギニア	03-3454-7801	
Paraguay パラグアイ	03-5570-4307	
Peru ペルー	03-3406-4240	
Philippines フィリピン	03-3496-2731	
Poland ポーランド	03-3711-5224	

Portugal ポルトガル	03-3400-7907	
Qatar カタール	03-3446-7561	
Romania ルーマニア	03-3479-0311	
Russia ロシア連邦	03-3583-4224	
Rwanda ルワンダ	03-3486-7800	
Saudi Arabia サウジアラビア	03-3589-5241	
Senegal セネガル	03-3464-8451	
Singapore シンガポール	03-3586-9111	
Spain スペイン	03-3583-8531	
Sri Lanka スリランカ	03-3585-7431	
Sudan スーダン	03-3406-0811	
Sweden スウェーデン	03-5562-5050	
Switzerland スイス	03-3473-0121	
Syria シリア	03-3586-8977	
Tanzania タンザニア	03-3425-4531	

Thailand タイ	03-3441-7352
Tunisia チュニジア	03-3353-4111
Turkey トルコ	03-3470-5131
U.A.E. アラブ首長国連邦	03-5489-0804
United Kingdom イギリス	03-3265-5511
Uruguay ウルグアイ	03-3486-1888
U.S.A. アメリカ合衆国	03-3224-5000
Vatican City ローマ法王庁	03-3263-6851
Venezuela ベネズエラ	03-3409-1501
Viet Nam ベトナム	03-3466-3311
Yemen イエメン	03-3499-7151
Yugoslavia ユーゴスラビア	03-3447-3571
Zaire ザイール	03-3423-3981
Zambia ザンビア	03-3445-1041
Zimbabwe ジンバブエ	03-3280-0331

Airlines
航空会社

Aeroflot Russian Int'l Airlines (SU)	3434-9681	Japan Air System (JD)　日本エアシステム	
アエロフロート・ロシア国際航空		Int'l 国際	3438-1155
Air France (AF)　エールフランス	3475-2211	Domestic 国内	3432-6111
Air India (AI)　エア・インディア	3214-1981	Japan Asia Airways (EG)　日本アジア航空	3455-7511
Airlanka (UL)　エアランカ	3573-4261	KLM Royal Dutch Airlines (KL)	3216-0771
Air Nauru (ON)　エア・ナウル	3581-9271	KLM オランダ航空	
Air New Zealand (TE)	3287-1641	Korean Air (KE)　大韓航空	3211-3311
ニュージーランド航空		Lufthansa German Airlines (LH)	3580-2111
Alitalia Airlines (AZ)　アリタリア航空	3580-2242	ルフトハンザ・ドイツ航空	
All Nippon Airways (NH)　全日空		Malaysian Airline System (MH)	3503-5961
Int'l 国際	3272-1212	マレーシア航空	
Domestic 国内	5489-8800	Nothwest Airlines (NW)	3432-6000
American Airlines (AA)　アメリカン航空	3214-2111	ノースウエスト・オリエント航空	
Biman Bangladesh Airlines (BG)	3593-1252	Pakistan Int'l Airlines (PK)	3216-6511
バングラディシュ航空		パキスタン国際航空	
British Airways (BA)　英国航空	3593-8811	Philippine Airlines (PR)　フィリピン航空	3593-2421
Canadian Airlines Int'l (CP)	3281-7426	Qantas Airways (QF)	3593-7000
カナディアン航空		カンタス・オーストラリア航空	
Cathay Pacific Airways (CX)	3504-1531	Sabena Belgian World Airlines (SN)	3585-6151
キャセイ・パシフィック航空		サベナベルギー航空	
China Airlines (CI)　中華航空	3436-1661	Scandinavian Airlines (SK)	3503-8101
Civil Aviation of China (CA)　中国民航	3505-2021	スカンジナビア航空	
Delta Air Lines (DL)　デルタ航空	3213-8781	Singapore Airlines (SQ)　シンガポール航空	3213-3431
Egypt Air (MS)　エジプト航空	3211-4521	Swiss Air Transport (SR)　スイス航空	3212-1011
Finnair (AY)　フィンランド航空	3222-6801	Thai Airways Int'l (TG)　タイ国際航空	3503-3311
Garuda Indonesian Airways (GA)	3593-1181	United Airlines (UA)　ユナイテッド航空	3817-4411
ガルーダ・インドネシア航空		UTA French Airlines (UT)	3593-0773
Iberia Airlines (IB)　イベリア航空	3582-3631	UTA フランス航空	
Iran Air (IR)　イラン航空	3586-2101	Varig Brazilian Airlines (RG)	3211-6751
Iraqi Aiways (IA)　イラク航空	3586-5801	ヴァリグ・ブラジル航空	
Japan Airlines (JL)　日本航空			
Int'l 国際	3457-1181		
Domestic 国内	3456-2111		

TOKYO
A Bilingual Atlas

With over 48 bilingual maps, this indexed atlas is the essential survival guide for finding one's way around Tokyo.

Paperback; 154 pp; 151 mm x 213 mm

KYOTO-OSAKA
A Bilingual Atlas

The first bilingual reference for the Kansai region. 36 maps of all major metropolitan areas, transportation, and tourist areas.

Paperback; 96 pp; 151 mm x 213 mm

JAPAN : A Bilingual Atlas

The entire country of Japan, from Hokkaido to Okinawa, in more than 50 color maps.

Paperback; 128 pp; 151 mm x 213 mm

TOKYO: A Bilingual Map

A fold-out wall map of central Tokyo, plus detailed maps of major downtown areas.

Folder: 111 mm x 228 mm, Map: 611 mm x 840 mm

TOKYO METROPOLITAN AREA: A Bilingual Map

A fold-out wall map of the Kanto region, plus area maps of cities outside of central Tokyo.

Folder: 111 mm x 218 mm, Map: 606 mm x 856 mm

KYOTO-OSAKA: A Bilingual Map

A fold-out wall map of the Kansai region, including Kobe, Nagoya and Nara.

Folder: 111 mm x 228 mm, Map: 611 mm x 840 mm

JAPAN: A Bilingual Map

A fold-out national map indicating major travel routes, plus detailed maps of seven major metropolitan areas.

Folder: 138 mm x 264 mm, Map: 770 mm x 1058 mm

Routes to Airports 空港への交通

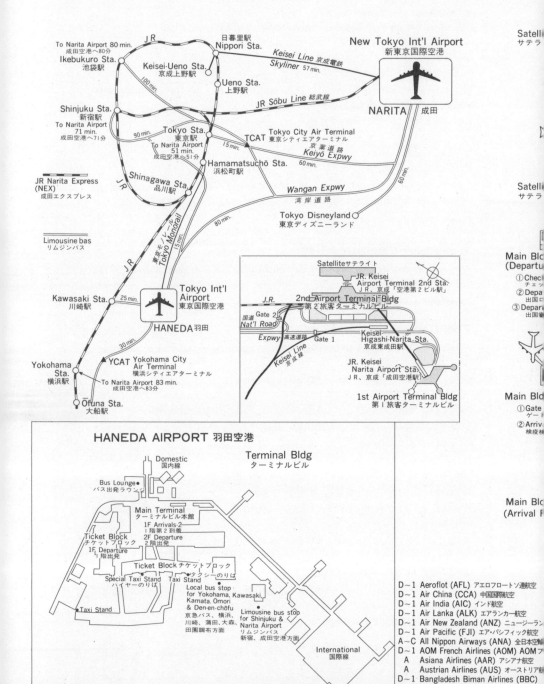

2nd Airport Terminal Bldg 第二旅客ターミナルビル

Departure Lounge 出発ラウンジ

Duty free shop 免税店

Play Room プレイルーム

Shuttle Stop シャトル乗降場

Arrival Concourse 到着コンコース

Information counter インフォメーションカウンター

Connecting Lounge 乗継客用ラウンジ

Connecting Lounge 乗継客用ラウンジ

Refresh room リフレッシュルーム

Audio room オーディオルーム

Duty free shop 免税店

Duty free shop 免税店

Duty free shop 免税店

■ Limousine bus リムジンバス
▲ Other bus その他バス

A B C D　E F G H　I J K L

B73　B72　B71　Shuttle Stop シャトル乗降場　A61　A62　A63　A64

Arrival Immigration 入国審査場

Domestic Terminal 国内線ターミナル

■ Limousine bus リムジンバス
▲ Other bus その他バス

Concourse コンコース

Baggage Clain 手荷物引渡所

Arrival Customs 税関検査場

Arrival Lobby 到着ロビー

Domestic counter 国内線チェックインカウンター

1st Airport Terminal Bldg 第一旅客ターミナルビル

South Wing 南ウイング

Restaurant レストラン

Shop 売店

■ Limousine bus リムジンバス
▲ Other bus その他バス

Temporary Baggage Check 手荷物一時預り所

4F 4階
① Check-in counter チェックインカウンター
② Departure lobby 出発ロビー
③ Charged waiting lounge 有料待合室
④ Information counter インフォメーションカウンター

Satellite サテライト

South Wing 南ウイング

Duty free shop 免税店

Service Center サービスセンター

Duty free shop 免税店

3F 3階
① Departures Quarantine 検疫検査場
② Departures Customs 税関検査場
③ Departures Immigration 出国審査場
④ Departure waiting lounge 出国待合室

South Wing 南ウイング

Restaurant レストラン

■ Limousine bus リムジンバス
▲ Other bus その他バス

Information Counter インフォメーションカウンター

Charged waiting room 有料待合室

1F 1階 (Arrival Floor 到着階)
① Arrival lobby 到着ロビー　② Arrival Customs 税関検査場
③ Baggage Clain 手荷物引渡所
④ Temporary Baggage check 手荷物一時預り所

Air France (AFR) エールフランス国営航空
Alitalia (AZA) アリタリア航空
American Airlines (AAL) アメリカン航空
British Airways (BAW) 英国航空
Canadian Pacific Airlines (CDN) カナディアン航空
Cathay Pacific Airways (CPA) キャセイ・パシフィック航空
Finnair (FIN) フィンランド航空
Korean Air Lines (KAL) 大韓航空
Lufthansa German Airlines (DLH) ルフトハンザ・ドイツ航空
Nothwest Airlines (NWA) ノースウエスト航空
Scandinavian Airlines (SAS) スカンジナビア航空
Singapore Airlines (SIA) シンガポール航空
Swissair (SWR) スイス航空
UTA French Airlines (UTA) UTAフランス航空
United Airlines (UAL) ユナイテッド航空
Vergin Atlantic Airways (VIR) ヴァージン・アトランティック航空
Varig Brazilian Airlines (VRG) ヴァリグ・ブラジル航空

1 China Eastern Airlines (CES) 中国東方航空		
1 Continental Airlines (COA) コンチネンタル航空		
1 Continental Air Micronesia (COA) コンチネンタルミクロネシア航空	D~1 Japan Asia Airways (JAA) 日本アジア航空	
1 Delta Airlines (DAL) デルタ航空	D~1 KLM Royal Dutch Airlines (KLM) KLMオランダ航空	
1 Egypt Air (MSR) エジプト航空	D~1 Malaysian Airline System (MAS) マレーシア航空	
1 Garuda Indonesian Airways (GIA) ガルーダ・インドネシア航空	D~1 Olympic Airways (OAL) オリンピック航空	
1 Iberia Airlines of Spain (IBE) イベリア航空	D~1 Pakistan International Airlines (PIA) パキスタン航空	
1 Iran Air (IRA) イラン航空	D~1 Philippine Airlines (PAL) フィリピン航空	
1 Iraqi Airways (IAW) イラク航空	A Sabena Belgian Airlines (SAB) サベナ・ベルギー航空	
1 Japan Air Lines (JAL) 日本航空	D~1 Thai Airways Int'l (THA) タイ国際航空	
1 Japan Air System (JAS) 日本エアシステム	A Turkish Airlines (THY) トルコ航空	